'I HAD TONS OF ACNE AND MUCUS. I MET SOME RANDOM GIRL ON A BUS WHO TOLD ME TO QUIT DAIRY AND ALL THOSE SYMPTOMS WOULD GO AWAY THREE DAYS LATER. BY GOD, SHE WAS RIGHT.'

WOODY 'MUCUS' HARRELSON

にきび

VEGAN

T I M A N D E R S O N

JAPANEASY

簡単日本食

CLASSIC & MODERN VEGAN JAPANESE
RECIPES TO COOK AT HOME
おいしい

Hardie Grant

BOOKS

BASIC SEASONINGS & SAUCES

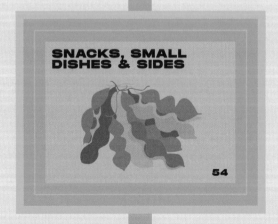

SNACKS, SMALL DISHES & SIDES

BIG DISHES

BIG RICE & NOODLE DISHES

DESSERTS & DRINKS

コンテンツ

INTRODUCTION

JAPANESE CUISINE: FATTY TUNA!
WAGYU BEEF! DRIED FISH! PORK BROTH!
FRIED CHICKEN! SQUID GUTS! EGGS!
EGGS, EVERYWHERE! IT'S A MINEFIELD
FOR MINDFUL VEGANS.

OR SO IT SEEMS. Of course, there are many Japanese delicacies that are off-limits for anyone who refrains from animal products. But Japanese cuisine in general is actually quite vegan-friendly – an enormous amount of Japanese food is inherently vegan, and much more can be made vegan with just a simple substitution or two. And it's not just austere, traditional Buddhist-temple fare (although that is very lovely indeed); you can enjoy the same big, bold, salty-sweet-spicy-rich-umami flavours of modern Japanese soul food without so much as glancing down the meat and dairy aisles.

Japanese dishes are often plant-based to begin with, since meat and milk were used sparingly throughout much of Japanese history, and most of Japan's oh-so satisfying seasonings are based on naturally vegan fermented soybean and rice products. Yes, fish is an issue – particularly the ubiquitous *dashi* that forms the basis of so many Japanese dishes – but this is easily replaced with mushroom- and seaweed-based versions that are just as delicious.

But let me be clear: this book won't teach you how to make joyless 'vegan versions' of Japanese meat and fish dishes, because they wouldn't be good, and there's no need to! Instead, this book will tap into Japan's rich culture of cookery that's already vegan or very nearly vegan, so there are no sad substitutes and no shortcomings of flavour.

PLUS you'll see that Japanese food isn't just vegan-friendly – it's also easy! Really, truly, embarassingly easy. So if you're new to veganism, new to Japanese cooking, new to both, or you just want to expand your meat-free repertoire, this is the book for you!

LET'S CHARGE VALIANTLY FORTH

BANZAI!!!

AND COOK VEGAN THE JAPANEASY WAY!!!

CONFESSION

告白

I'M NOT VEGAN. OR AT LEAST, NOT OFFICIALLY. BUT I AM VEGAN FREQUENTLY AND ACCIDENTALLY.

Let me explain. I do eat meat and cheese and eggs, and I wear leather. (What can I say? I look good in chaps.) I grew up in Wisconsin – 'America's Dairyland'* – where I'm pretty sure it's against the law to be vegan in public. So, for better or worse, cheese and sausages are in my blood. And, while I've never had any scorn for veganism the way some of my meat-eating brethren do, it's just never been for me. I don't generally do well with restrictions, dietary or otherwise, primarily because I have no impulse control.

However, something weird happened over the past few years: I became kinda-sorta vegan by accident. In 2015, I opened my restaurant, Nanban, and for many months I was working there between 60 and 100 hours a week, so I rarely cooked at home. I had to change the way I shopped, since the fresh food I bought would often spoil before I had a chance to cook it. I wound up buying meat and fish very rarely and instead stocked up on things that would last, like root vegetables, frozen peas and spinach, tinned beans and tomatoes, and lots of pasta, noodles and rice. I still bought cheese and eggs, and cured meat and fish like bacon and anchovies, but I didn't actually use them that much. Over time, I realised that most of my cooking had become largely vegetarian and sometimes entirely vegan – and I didn't even miss the meat and dairy. Hell, I hardly even noticed it was gone.

How could this be?! I was raised on bratwurst and frozen custard. If you cut me, I bleed fondue. The traditional dress of Wisconsin includes giant 'cheesehead' hats made out of orange polyurethane foam.** I honestly think I didn't go a single day without eating meat until I moved to California when I was 18. Yet there I was, in my South London flat, cooking vegan food and happily devouring it like some kind of hipster jackass. What would my parents say? What the hell happened to me?!

In short: Japan happened. I've been obsessed with Japanese food since I was a teenager, and I lived in Japan for two years after studying Japanese food history in college. Now, some of you may already be aware that Japan is not a place that is particularly amenable to vegans, or even vegetarians. I actually dated a vegetarian for a few months in Japan, and going out with her was fraught with prohibitive complications. First of all, there were loads of places we simply couldn't go because they specialised in just one meaty or fishy thing, like sushi or grilled chicken or pork broth ramen. And then there were cultural differences regarding the definition of 'vegetarian' (and the definition of 'meat') that made it tricky to ensure that a supposedly 'meat-free' dish would be prepared without fish, or even chicken or pork (!). A friend of mine once joked that a common exchange between a vegetarian and a server in a Japanese restaurant might go like this:

'IS THIS VEGETARIAN?'

'YES.'

'DOES IT HAVE BACON IN IT?'

'YES.'

So it wasn't in Japan where I learned to appreciate vegetarian food in and of itself, because there wasn't that much of it going. But what I did learn was how awesome Japanese seasonings are, and how to combine and layer them to create wonderfully more-ish and satisfying meals, with or without meat. This is how so much of my cooking at home wound up accidentally vegan; when you have such fantastic, flavoursome ingredients at your disposal – things like tangy miso, savoury shiitake mushrooms and zingy ponzu, to name a few – then who needs meat? Japanese flavours are just that awesome. And not only that, but Japanese home cooking is usually really quick and easy; despite its reputation, most Japanese food doesn't require lots of prep or tricky techniques. It's so easy a (vegan) monkey could make it.

ビーガンモンキー

VEGAN MONKEY

* Not a joke – this is Wisconsin's actual nickname.
** Also (sadly) not a joke.

UMAMI DEAREST
MEATY FLAVOUR WITHOUT THE MEAT

旨味

One of the reasons Japanese cuisine has become so popular around the world is because of its ability to deliver rich, substantial, satisfying flavours even in lighter dishes that don't necessarily contain meat. This is largely because Japanese ingredients are rather good at delivering *umami*.

UMAMI is a basic taste; the best English translation we have for it is 'savouriness'. However, despite its simplicity, it's often made out to be something mysterious and inscrutable, erroneously described by charlatan chefs and Japanese gastro-nationalists as a perfectly balanced combination of other tastes, only attainable by master craftsmen. In an interview in *The New Yorker*, the founder of the Californian nü-burger chain 'Umami Burger' explained umami as 'an over-all harmonious state of perfection where the ingredients come together, a really rounded and harmonious dish. [The Japanese] have a sort of zen way of looking at it'.

This is wrong. It's as wrong as saying that salty is the combination of sweet and sour. It's as wrong as saying that bitterness is an over-all bad-feeling frowny-face flavour. It's as wrong as saying that 1 + 1 = 4. It is categorically, decidedly, unquestionably wrong. It is a vortex of wrongness, dark and deep and swirling, leading into a wormhole of infinite stupidity. UMAMI IS A BASIC TASTE, as simple and straightforward as sweetness, saltiness, bitterness or sourness. So why is it so commonly misapprehended?

It could be because umami tends to be more subtle than the other tastes. You may not always notice umami, but you'd likely notice its absence. It's pretty rare to hear someone exclaim, 'Oh wow, that's so UMAMI!', and you'll probably never send a dish back at a restaurant because it's *too umami*, but food that lacks sufficient umami is just blah. Hollow. Insipid. The opposite of more-ish (less-ish?). Umami really is important, even if it often goes unnoticed. And many people think that it's hard to work a sufficiently deep, satisfying flavour into dishes without meat or fish, but as anybody who has enjoyed a lovely bowl of pasta with a rich and tangy tomato sauce can tell you, that's not really true. Umami has a huge range of sources and, actually, most of them are plants.

There are three main compounds that deliver umami: inosinate, guanylate and glutamate.

INOSINATE is abundant in meat and fish, and is a key component of the 'meaty' flavour of meat (along with one of my other favourite compounds, the 'beefy meaty peptide'*). In Japanese cuisine, inosinate mainly comes from katsuobushi, the dried, smoked and fermented tuna flakes that are used to flavour a wide variety of dishes. Even though it's usually derived from fish, inosinate isn't entirely off the table for vegans, because it can also be found in nori seaweed – the same stuff you use to wrap sushi.

Additionally, the closely related compound called **GUANYLATE** can step in to provide a massive umami boost in lieu of inosinate. And the good news is, guanylate is found in high concentrations in plants and fungi, especially mushrooms and *especially* dried mushrooms, which are hugely important in Japanese cuisine.

Last, but certainly not least, there is **GLUTAMATE**, the most common umami compound. You may recognise it as part of monosodium glutamate, or MSG...

MSG MYTH MONSTER!

OH NO! IT'S THE

モンスター

MSG MONSTER

RAAAR!
MSG IS AN ARTIFICIAL
CHEMICAL FLAVOURING!

You've got it all wrong! MSG, or its conjugate base, glutamate, is actually found in abundance in a wide variety of natural ingredients, including tomatoes, peas, walnuts, seaweed, green tea and human breast milk, as well as in many traditional food products like soy sauce, yeast extract, cheese, wine and miso. Even manufactured MSG is primarily derived from bacterial fermentation, not through chemical synthesis. Frankly, it's far more 'natural' than many vegan products out there (I'm looking at you, Tofurkey).

GRRR! MSG CAUSES MIGRAINES, SEIZURES, DIARRHOEA, ALZHEIMER'S AND DOZENS OF OTHER NEGATIVE HEALTH EFFECTS!

Not true, Myth Monster! Countless peer-reviewed studies conducted over the past several decades have failed to provide any evidence that MSG causes short-term or long-term health problems, including so-called 'Chinese restaurant syndrome', a vaguely racist and poorly defined suite of symptoms such as headaches, feeling flushed and perspiration. Anecdotal evidence does suggest that MSG sensitivity may exist, but no experiments have actually confirmed it. My conjecture is that self-reported MSG issues are actually caused by something else commonly found in tandem with MSG, such as an undiagnosed soy or wheat allergy, or hypertension brought on by too much salt. If you're absolutely convinced that MSG gives you trouble, then by all means do avoid it – but bear in mind that you're inevitably consuming it in other forms, such as soy sauce, ketchup or pickles.

AAARGH! MSG IS USED
AS A CHEAT BY INEPT COOKS OR
UNSCRUPULOUS MANUFACTURERS TO
MAKE BAD INGREDIENTS TASTE GOOD!

No! Well, yes... sometimes. MSG can indeed be added to foods that are otherwise largely devoid of flavour to make them palatable – instant ramen, crisps (chips) and stock (bouillon) cubes are notorious for this. (By the way, if you see 'yeast extract' in a list of ingredients, that's basically an indirect way of adding MSG.) But MSG is just a seasoning, and while it can be used to cover for flavour deficiencies, it can also be used to enhance flavours that are already there, just like salt and sugar can. Let me put it this way: a perfectly ripe tomato or avocado may taste good on its own, but it will taste *great* with a little sprinkling of sea salt and/ or MSG.

This is all just to say that MSG is harmless, and helpful! It's part of what makes so much Japanese food taste so good – Japanese seasonings are naturally chock-full of it, especially soy sauce, miso and various seaweeds. So, if you're eating Japanese food, you're eating MSG, whether you're adding it directly or not. None of the recipes in this book call for pure MSG, but if you want to use it, that would be absolutely in keeping with real Japanese home cooking; on kitchen tables and countertops in Japan you'll frequently find a little jar of *ajishio*, so-called 'flavour salt', which is actually just MSG.

But it's not just about umami. The deliciousness of Japanese food also comes from sugar, salt, acid and the distinctive *Japaneseness* of certain ingredients – of which you won't need very many to get started.

---

*This actually is what it's called, sometimes shortened to BMP or referred to as 'delicious peptide'.

THE **VEGAN JAPANESE** LARDER
SEVEN ESSENTIAL ITEMS

I believe we are living in a golden age of grocery shopping. In 15 years or so, catastrophic climate change will cause worldwide crop failures and a collapse of international trade and logistics, but until then, it's one big **INGREDIENTS PARTY!** Thanks to globalisation and the marvels of the information age, it is truly amazing what you can get at ordinary supermarkets these days – everything from ackee to za'atar. You'll only need the following seven Japanese ingredients to cook most of the recipes in this book, and you should have little trouble finding them in the 'world foods' aisle of your local grocery store. But if you do have trouble, and you don't live anywhere near an Asian food shop, remember you can always buy ingredients online. ~~Some of you~~ Almost all of you probably bought this book on Amazon – and you can actually order Japanese ingredients from the very same site, if you are so inclined.

You may not be cooking Japanese food every day – that's cool, I don't take it personally. But these are very versatile ingredients, perfectly compatible with all sorts of cooking, so you don't have to worry about buying them only to see them collect dust in the pantry. I've included a few tips on how to use each one even if you're not making Japanese dishes.

1 | SOY SAUCE

Soy sauce is one of the most common and beloved Japanese ingredients there is. I grew up with it – one of the largest Kikkoman factories outside of Japan is in Wisconsin (chosen for our abundance of delicious soybeans and wheat), so we always had some in the pantry. But really, it should be familiar to pretty much everybody, and you probably have a bottle at home already. There are several varieties available, but do try to use a Japanese one rather than a Chinese one – the flavour can be remarkably different. And check the label! A good soy sauce should be made from water, soybeans, wheat and salt – not caramel colouring, acidifiers or flavour enhancers. There's nothing inherently wrong with these things, but soy sauces that contain them tend to taste somewhat watery and sharp compared to a 'naturally brewed' soy sauce. You may also encounter (or already own) tamari, brewed with little or no wheat so its flavour is much more intense. Tamari is great for pairing with stronger-flavoured ingredients, such as onions, mushrooms, root vegetables or chocolate, but it shouldn't be your go-to soy sauce as it has such a dominant flavour.

Non-Japanese uses: Put it in anything with big, strong flavours where you want to amplify umami – it's great in tomato sauce, hearty soups and stews, baked beans or simple vinaigrettes.

2 | SAKE

SAKE

Sake is kind of difficult to describe, but easy to drink, and even easier to cook with. In food, it functions like white wine, with similar levels of acidity and sweetness (and aroma-boosting alcohol) but with a more savoury character. The range of flavours in sake is broad, but most supermarkets only sell one kind, and that one kind will almost inevitably be basic plonk sake. Which is fine – actually, ideal – for cooking. Premium sake is usually delicate, fruity and floral, while B-grade sake is more earthy and rich, with funky notes of fermented rice, sourdough and mushrooms. These aromas are by-products of *aspergillus oryzae*, or kōji – the 'national fungus' of Japan, also used to make soy sauce, miso, mirin and rice vinegar. Kōji delivers a uniquely 'Japanese' flavour, and sake delivers one of the purest expressions of kōji. It's subtle, but it's also essential.

Non-Japanese uses: Well, you can drink it, of course! But if you do, just make sure you keep it in the refrigerator once it's opened, and drink it within a week or it will go sour. Otherwise, you can treat it like white wine – it's especially nice in a risotto, or add a generous glug to some chilli, garlic, capers and basil that have been sautéed in olive oil for a simple and delicious pasta sauce.

3 | MIRIN

Mirin is kind of like sake but with far more sugar, so the finished product is akin to a sweet, viscous wine. Most commercially available mirin these days aren't what's called 'true mirin', but are actually a low-alcohol rice-based syrup – and this stuff is totally fine for everyday cooking, and a fraction of the price of the 'real' mirin because it avoids both

Japanese and international alcohol duties. It lends dishes a soft, honeyed sweetness and is an essential component of the sweet-and-salty flavour profile that makes so much Japanese food so irresistible.

Non-Japanese uses: Many dishes benefit from a touch of sweetness that mirin can provide, especially dishes from other parts of East Asia – mirin works well in Thai, Vietnamese and Korean sauces and marinades to balance their acidity and spice. But one of my favourite uses for mirin is to simply drizzle it over vegetables for roasting. The mirin helps the vegetables caramelise beautifully and heightens the flavour of things that are already sweet, such as pumpkin, swede (rutabaga) or sweet potatoes.

4 | RICE VINEGAR

Rice vinegar is another offshoot on the sake family tree – it's simply sake or a sake-like rice liquor refermented into vinegar. It offers a bright, clean acidity with a little bit of sake's malty sweetness and umami, and while Japanese food isn't often outright sour, rice vinegar is essential in balancing the sweetness of many dishes and providing a zippy, mouthwatering tang. As with soy sauce, it's best to get a Japanese one as it will have a slightly different flavour profile from Chinese versions.

Non-Japanese uses: Basically everything. Rice vinegar has such a nice flavour, but it's not too assertive, so it's my go-to vinegar. Use it in place of cider or white wine vinegar.

5 | MISO

Miso, of soup fame, is a paste made from fermented soybeans, rice, and sometimes other grains. Its flavour runs the gamut from light, fresh and sweet to rich, complex and intense (and always quite salty). It's especially useful in vegan cooking because it mimics some of the tangy, fruity flavours you get from aged cheese. There are two broad categories of miso: white and red. The former is made with a higher proportion of rice to soybeans and it is not aged very long, so its flavour is lighter, while the latter is made with more soy beans and aged at least six months, but sometimes much longer, so it is more rich and savoury. You may find red miso that has been aged a *very* long time, such as the famous Hatchō miso, with a deep walnut-wood colour and a profound flavour like kalamata olives and balsamic vinegar. Buy a few different kinds to acquaint yourself with their flavours (they last forever in the refrigerator) and soon you'll be adding miso to everything. I know a few people who just have it spread on toast, like Marmite.

Non-Japanese uses: Like soy sauce, miso can be added to just about anything to enhance its umami, but its flavour is more distinct, so you may want to use it more sparingly. It's awesome in a marinade for anything grilled, because when it chars and caramelises the flavour becomes even more intense and complex, so slather it onto tofu, tomatoes, sweetcorn or broccoli and give them a good blast under the grill (broiler).

6 | DASHI

Dashi is a light broth that provides the foundation for so many Japanese dishes, made by infusing *kombu* (dried kelp) into warm water along with *katsuobushi*, shavings of skipjack tuna loins that have been smoked, fermented and dried until they resemble chunks of driftwood. Katsuobushi is one of the most important, fundamental and irreplaceable flavours in Japanese gastronomy and there really is no substitute and – oh DAMMIT, this is a vegan book... hang on let me backtrack a bit. Katsuobushi is an important flavour in a lot of Japanese food, but not all Japanese food, and you can still create dishes with a solid Japanese flavour and lots of umami without it. In fact, dashi at its most basic is made from just kombu, which has enough naturally occurring MSG in it to provide a sufficiently umami flavour to any dish. Your best bet for easy, delicious and inexpensive dashi is to buy instant **kombu dashi powder**, a Japanese home-kitchen essential. But dashi is also dead easy to make from scratch – and you can build upon it with dried mushrooms or other types of seaweed to make truly exquisite dashi that's totally vegan – check the recipes on pages 33–34.

Non-Japanese uses: Get to know dashi and you'll never use vegetable stock again. It's so much more flavourful and so much easier to make, and if you make it from scratch it won't have any salt in it, so you have more control over your seasoning. It is fantastic as a base for soups and sauces or as a cooking liquid for rice or other grains.

7 | RICE

More often than not, Japanese meals are just not complete without rice. In fact, the Japanese word for meal is the same for cooked rice: *gohan.* And it has to be Japanese rice, not just some pouch of Uncle Ben's you have in the back of the cupboard, otherwise I will call the Japanese Culinary Authenticity Police to come and kick your door down and have you arrested for grand rice larceny. Just kidding! Following a 2015 decision by the International Court of Justice, the JCAP have no jurisdiction outside Japan. But still, to me having Japanese food with non-Japanese rice is just plain weird, so go buy some and then learn to cook it nicely (it's easy – see page 26).

Non-Japanese uses: Japanese rice is short-grained and slightly sticky, so it isn't quite right with South Asian dishes, but it works reasonably well with Chinese and Korean food, and it's perfect for risotto or rice pudding. You can also use it to try to dry out your phone after you accidentally drop it in the toilet.

ELEVEN MORE
LOVELY VEGAN
JAPANESE THINGS
YOU MAY WANT TO GET

These ingredients aren't what you might call essentials, but they're good to have on hand for when a sudden Japanese craving strikes. Just like the seven ingredients on the previous page, pretty much all of them should be available at your nearest big supermarket, but if not they will be easy to find at Asian stores or online.

1 | TOFU (DUH)

If you're a vegan veteran then you will be no stranger to tofu. And even if you're not, you probably already have an opinion about it. For something so bland and benign it seems to evoke very strong reactions. I'm not that passionate one way or another about tofu, although I do have a fondness for the silky silkenness of **silken tofu**, the one that comes in little Tetrapaks and has a texture like crème caramel. But **firm (cotton) tofu**, sometimes sold as 'block' tofu, is nice as well, especially if it's fried to make its surface more porous, so it absorbs flavourful sauces like a sponge. As a 'meat substitute' I think tofu is rubbish, especially when you can just use hearty vegetables to give dishes substance and flavour. But sometimes you need the soft blandness of tofu, whether it's to create a light and delicate dish, such as Fried Tofu in Dashi (page 98), or to counter the intensity of a spicy sauce or broth, as in Kimchi and Tofu Gyoza (page 103) or Tofu Patties (page 74).

2 | MUSHROOMS

The first mushrooms you should buy if you're setting off on a Japanese food journey are **dried shiitake**. You can get these at normal grocery stores, but you're better off buying them at an Asian market if you can, because they are much cheaper there. Dried shiitake are great because you get two uses out of them: first to make a dashi, and then, once they're rehydrated, as the mushrooms themselves. The drying process concentrates their flavour and creates more of the umami compound guanylate, so they're super meaty and intense. Fresh shiitake are nice as well, and of course there are a wide range of Japanese mushrooms now available at supermarkets, like spindly **enoki**, toothsome **eringi** and nutty **shimeji**. But even good old button mushrooms or chestnut (cremini) mushrooms are lovely, and I think they have a special affinity with soy sauce and sake.

3 | SEAWEED

Peruse the aisles of a Japanese food store and you'll find dozens of kinds of delicious seaweeds, but the three you should start with (and the only three you're likely to find at a supermarket) are kombu, nori and wakame. **Kombu** is dried kelp, used most commonly to make dashi (pages 33–34), but which can also be rehydrated and shredded for use in salads or pickles. **Nori** are dark-green dried sheets of laver, mainly used in sushi rolls, but also flaked or shredded and used as a garnish. **Wakame** are the supple, spinach-y leaves you find in a bowl of miso soup, or in light, fresh salads, such as Cucumber and Wakame with Seasoned Vinegar on page 86. Because they're dried, they last forever, so stock up!

4 | PICKLES

Pickles are a great way to introduce a distinctly Japanese flavour to a meal, as a garnish or as a side dish. A bowl of rice is just a bowl of rice, but a bowl of rice with Japanese pickles on top is a *Japanese* bowl of rice. **Pickled ginger** is perhaps the most common, and it comes in two forms: *gari*, the thinly-sliced pale pink or yellow stuff is sweeter and pretty much exclusively used as a garnish for sushi, while *beni shōga*, the julienned bright red stuff, is used as a topping for strongly flavoured dishes like yakisoba or fried rice. Some supermarkets sell a few other kinds of pickles as well, and Asian stores should sell quite a wide variety, but if you can't find any, you can make them yourself – check the recipes on pages 56–60.

5 | NOODLES

On a list of things that bring me joy, noodles claim the number one spot. I mean, sure, I love my cat and my baby, but I also love noodles. I don't know what it is about noodles – it's something about the way they can be hoovered up with such gusto, the way they break so satisfyingly between the teeth, the way they steadily fill your tummy like you're stuffing a pillow. Noodles are just the best.

My favourite are **ramen**: wheat noodles made with alkaline water to give them a sprightly bite, sturdy and strong even after a long bath in hot broth. **Soba** are fantastic as well, made with buckwheat flour for a nutty flavour and a brittle al dente texture. **Udon** are my least favourite: the doughiest, chewiest noodles, but they do have an almost dumpling-like quality that can be supremely comforting. And then there are **somen**: exquisitely delicate and thin noodles, best served cold to maintain their texture. Most Japanese noodles are sold dried – in fact, I have never seen soba and somen sold fresh, except in Japan. Ramen is better fresh or frozen, if you can get it, and the only one I'd advise to *only* buy fresh or frozen is udon – the dried stuff isn't thick enough. And as for soba, there are some weird so-called 'soba' products in supermarkets these days that I think are made from buckwheat starch rather than buckwheat flour, so they're a funny shape and have a strange, chewy texture. Soba should be perfectly straight, thin, square-cut and visibly grainy and grey from the buckwheat. They usually come in cute little paper-bound bundles. Learn to distinguish soba from faux-ba to avoid noodle disappointment.

6 | TOASTED SESAME SEEDS

In Japanese cuisine, sesame seeds are almost invariably toasted, which gives them a lovely, rich, nutty flavour and a crisp texture. Toasting them yourself is easy – just put them in a dry frying pan (skillet) over a medium heat and cook, stirring very frequently, until they are golden brown and very aromatic. They release their flavour even more when ground to a coarse powder. You can also buy them pre-toasted, but to be honest I think these are better after a secondary toast at home anyway. So it's up to you.

7 | TOASTED SESAME OIL

Toasted sesame oil captures the heady aroma of roasted sesame seeds in convenient liquid form, and it's indispensible in Japanese soul food recipes such as 'Deep Roast' Sesame Dressing (page 42), Gyoza (pages 102–103) and Surprisingly Awesome One-Hour Spicy Sesame, Aubergine and Courgette Ramen (page 142). I don't know why, but I also find it to be an effective cure-all for flavour deficiencies; if a dish seems to be 'missing something', a drizzle of sesame oil and a pinch of sea salt will usually fix it.

8 | PANKO

Panko are Japanese breadcrumbs that have a light, airy texture and shard-like shape, which produce supremely crisp crusts. Most supermarkets sell it these days, but be warned that some 'own brand' panko have taken the coarseness of panko way too far, so they're more like breadchunks than breadcrumbs. This makes them difficult to work with and creates a clunky, dense, unpleasant end product, so it's better to buy a Japanese brand if you can.

9 | TONKATSU SAUCE

Tonkatsu sauce is a kind of Japanese brown sauce, often shortened to 'katsu sauce', or even just 'sauce' in Japan. It tastes quite similar to HP, but with a fruitier Worcestershire sauce-like flavour, more sweetness and more umami. You can buy it in some supermarkets – the most common brand is Bulldog, which is good – but it's also pretty easy to make yourself (page 47).

10 | SHICHIMI TŌGARASHI

Shichimi tōgarashi (or sometimes '*nanami tōgarashi*') means 'seven flavour chilli', and that's exactly what it is – a blend of chilli powder plus six other aromatic ingredients, usually black and white sesame seeds, nori, dried orange peel, dried ginger, Sichuan pepper, hemp seeds or white poppy seeds. It is sometimes sold as just 'tōgarashi', which is incorrect because that just means 'chilli', and sometimes as 'togorashi', which is even more incorrect, because that's not even a word. It's usually shortened to 'shichimi' in Japan, but whatever you call it, it's delicious – not just spicy but also fruity and nutty. It isn't used in that many recipes but it's good to have on hand as an all-purpose spicy seasoning – the combination of soy sauce and shichimi is kind of like the Japanese salt and pepper.

11 | YUZU JUICE

Yuzu: the one true king of citrus. A hybrid between the mandarin orange and the Ichang lemon, yuzu is a kind of über-fruit; it smells like lime, lemon and grapefruit all rolled into one, plus a distinctive herbaceous note reminiscent of thyme and pine needles. You can now buy yuzu juice in some supermarkets, but be prepared to shell out for it; the fruit is full of big seeds and light on juice, so it costs more than many single malt whiskies. Do buy some if you can, as it really is delicious, although it's far from essential. And avoid yuzu juice blends – they contain vinegar and other citrus fruits, and while they are cheaper, they don't actually represent good value because they come up short on aroma. If you're a yuzu sceptic, best to just stick with limes and lemons.

VEGAN STUFF

If you're already running around buying loads of new Japanese ingredients, it doesn't seem fair to make you go buy loads of new vegan ingredients as well. And besides, it's not really necessary. There are just a handful of recipes in this book that call for **mock meat** and **non-dairy cheese**, but in most cases you can leave these out and the recipes will still be good. You may also want to buy **egg replacer** for recipes that are breadcrumbed, because it's cheap and super-easy to use, but an alternative substitute can be found on page 46. Additionally, two ingredients I find incredibly useful for all sorts of cooking, but particularly in vegan recipes, are **mushroom ketchup** and **nutritional yeast** or **yeast extract**. Mushroom ketchup tastes a lot like Worcestershire sauce; it's just a fantastic flavour enhancer to have on hand, and it is essential in Tonkatsu Sauce (page 47) and Yakisoba Sauce. Nutritional yeast is sometimes sold as 'yeast flakes' and it has a really rich, nutty, almost cheesy flavour, while yeast extract (Marmite, Vegemite, etc.) delivers a massive, beefy umami hit, although it is extraordinarily salty and too much can be quite overpowering. A guy on Twitter told me that some yeast extracts contain the umami compound inosinate, which is usually only found in meat and fish derivatives. I don't know if that's true, but it would explain the full-on flavour boost these products provide. All of these are widely available at most major supermarkets, at health food stores and online.

SHŌJIN RYŌRI
JAPAN'S PLANT–BASED
BUDDHIST TEMPLE COOKING

Originally, when planning this book, I wanted to include recipes from *shōjin ryōri*, traditional Buddhist temple cooking. But the more I researched this cuisine, of which I had only the vaguest understanding, the more I realised I just couldn't include it in a book with 'easy' in its title. That's not because all *shōjin ryōri* dishes are difficult – quite the contrary, many of them are beautifully simple – but because they are intrinsically linked to bigger concepts of balance, spiritual well-being, asceticism, seasonality and mindfulness that I simply couldn't do justice to.

Having said that, some recipes in this book are not dissimilar from what you might be served at a Buddhist temple in Japan – these are the lighter dishes that showcase the inherent flavours of seasonal vegetables without the heavy use of seasonings. Try the Kale with Crushed Sesame (page 67), Squash Braised in Dashi (page 71), Fried Tofu in Dashi (page 98) or Mixed Vegetable Rice (page 165) if you want to experience some of the flavours you're likely to find in *shōjin ryōri*. Or better yet, just go to Japan. Flights are surprisingly cheap!

海藻

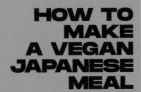

HOW TO MAKE A VEGAN JAPANESE MEAL

Japanese meals can have many different arrangements, from the elaborate multi-course feasts of *kaiseki* cuisine way down to just one big-ass bowl of ramen. In between there are all kinds of different combinations, which vary depending on the type of food and the occasion. One of the most important guiding principles in Japanese cooking is *ichijū sansai,* or 'one soup, three sides', a format that began as an element of complex pre-modern formal banqueting, but has been simplified and streamlined over time so it's now a commonplace serving style in Japanese homes. Even so, it's not quite as simple as it sounds – in addition to the 'three sides', a meal following this structure should also include a rice and pickles, so really you're looking at six dishes (!) in one meal. Granted, rice is hardly a dish, miso soup is super-quick (from a packet is fine), and the pickles can be shop-bought, but still, it's a bit much for a Tuesday evening, don't you think?

Luckily, this format is not always followed to the letter; it's more just something to keep in mind when you're planning a Japanese meal. The rice-soup-pickles combo is a great place to start, and in fact if you just make one dish to go with it – something substantial, like braised root vegetables or a hearty stir-fry – you're looking at a very balanced, satisfying dinner. But you don't always even need the soup and pickles; some dishes are meals in and of themselves, like the rice bowls on pages 160–168 or, of course, any dish based on noodles (pages 142–158). Sometimes these are served with sides, like pickles with a plate of curry, or gyoza with ramen, but those are more like bonuses, not integral parts of the meal.

This is all to say that there aren't really any rules – dishes can be mixed and matched or served on their own, however you see fit. I always think of two examples I encountered in Japan where traditional meal structures were thrown out the window. The first are ramen shops in Japan that serve rice – the carbohydrate double-down of noodles and rice together is kind of funny to me, but there are many people in Japan who simply feel a meal is not complete without rice, so rice they must have! And then there are the restaurants that only sell one thing; there was a gyoza shop in the city where I lived in Japan where you could go and just eat truckloads of gyoza until you were full. That's it. Just gyoza. No rice, no pickles, no salad, no nothing. The only side dish was beer.

All the recipes in this book tell you the amount of servings they provide, accounting for what kind of meal you may be making – i.e. some dishes may serve two people if served as a main course with little else, but they may serve four if you're preparing other things. But whatever sort of meal you're making, more often than not, you will need **RICE.** So, let's learn how to cook it!

25

紹介

HOW TO COOK JAPANESE RICE

DIFFICULTY More difficult than potatoes, but less difficult than bread

MAKES 4 SMALL SERVINGS, 2-3 GENEROUS SERVINGS, OR ENOUGH FOR 5-6 ONIGIRI (PAGE 64)

The road to good rice is paved with failure: so many chalky grains, mushy pastes and burned bottoms. A while back on Twitter someone posed the question 'what's the one thing in cooking you always screw up?' and numerous (skilled, professional) chefs responded: RICE. Cooking Japanese rice is particularly tricky because it's steamed, rather than boiled, which means the timings and measurements involved need to be a bit more precise. But once you have those timings and measurements nailed down, it's really very easy.

When you're shopping for Japanese rice, you'll probably come across something called 'sushi rice'. This is just Japanese rice, mislabelled. Sushi rice isn't a type of rice, it's Japanese rice that has been cooked and seasoned a certain way for making sushi (page 106). I have no idea why so many manufacturers have gone with such a confusing name, but there it is. Anyway, you're better off buying Japanese rice at an Asian supermarket if you can, because it will be much cheaper there.

You'll need a pan with a snug-fitting lid for this. Or a rice cooker! In fact, if you have a rice cooker, just ignore this recipe and do what the rice cooker says.

300 g (10½ oz/1½ cups) Japanese rice
390 ml/g (13¾ oz/1⅔ cups) water

The ratio of rice to water for any quantity of rice is 1:1.3 by weight (or 1:1.1 by volume). You'll need about 75 g (2½ oz/generous ⅓ cup) rice per serving – more like 100 g (3½ oz/½ cup) if the rice is the main part of the meal (such as in fried rice or rice bowls), but only 50–60 g (2 oz/¼ cup) if you're making rice balls or if you are not that carb-hungry. And it is better to do it by weight – scales are more accurate than cups or jugs, and this way you can measure everything directly into the pan you're using.

Weigh out the rice into a pan and wash it. Fill the pan with water, swish the grains around and massage them gently, then drain the water out. Repeat this process three or four times. This is to rinse off excess starch, which makes the rice pasty (that starch is basically rice flour, so when it cooks it forms a kind of sticky glue). Pour the measured water into the pan and swirl it around a bit so the grains redistribute and settle in an even layer. If you have time, let the rice soak for 15–30 minutes, which will help them cook more evenly. If you can't wait, don't worry – unsoaked rice will still be good.

Place the pan on a high heat* with the lid off and bring to the boil. Place the lid on the pan and turn the heat way down – maybe not all the way down, because the rice should still be bubbling away, but it should be pretty low. As the rice cooks, you should be able to hear it ticking away and see some steam escaping from the lid; if this isn't happening, turn up the heat a tiny bit. Set a timer for 15 minutes, then leave it to steam. Avoid the urge to remove the lid to check on the rice – it will be fine!

When the timer is up, turn off the heat and fluff the rice with chopsticks or a fork, using a slice-and-fold motion rather than a dig-and-scoop motion so you don't smash the grains. Put the lid back on the pan and wait another 5–10 minutes so the residual steam continues to soften the grains and loosen the stuck rice from the bottom of the pan. Finally, give the rice another gentle fluffing, then serve and enjoy!

* If you have an induction hob, start the rice off on a medium heat; high heat on induction is too quick and intense, which makes the rice stick and burn almost immediately. Use caution and let the water come to the boil slowly, stirring occasionally to make sure the grains aren't catching.

STORING AND REHEATING RICE

Conventional wisdom dictates that rice should not be reheated, for food safety reasons. This is weird and wrong. There's absolutely nothing dangerous about reheating rice, and in fact it reheats quite nicely in the microwave from chilled or frozen. What you really mustn't do is leave lukewarm rice out for too long; there's a kind of bacteria called *bacillus cereus* that creates spores that are often present in uncooked rice. These spores germinate between 10–50°C (50–122°F) and they aren't killed by reheating, even at temperatures above boiling. So, it isn't about the reheating – it's about the cooling. If you know you'll have leftover rice, get it chilled down as quickly as you can by leaving it uncovered in a shallow container in the refrigerator, then cover it and eat it within a few days. Or you can freeze it: divide cooked rice into individual portions in small containers or plastic bags, stash them in the freezer for up to 3 months, and simply microwave them for a minute or two to reheat.

COOK'S NOTES

- For deep-frying: use a neutral-flavoured vegetable oil such as rapeseed (canola) or sunflower. Use a very large, wide, deep pan; the maximum oil level should be 8 cm (3 in) below the top of the pan. Never add wet food to hot oil. Use a digital probe thermometer to check the oil temperature – these are widely available online, at kitchen stores and at some supermarkets. Oil from deep-frying can be re-used; once cooled, pass it through a sieve (fine-mesh strainer) and keep in an airtight container. Discard the oil when it is noticeably darker in colour.

- 'Oil' indicates neutral vegetable oil.

- 'Vinegar' indicates rice vinegar.

- Rice should be Japanese, Korean or Taiwanese short-grain rice.

- Soy sauce should be Japanese soy sauce, and not tamari, unless specified.

- 1 tbsp = 15 ml; 1 tsp = 5 ml.

- Use volume measurements or weight as the recipe indicates.

- Use fine salt unless sea salt flakes are specified.

- Use fresh ingredients unless frozen, dried or tinned are specified.

- Oven temperatures stated are for fan ovens.

BASIC SEAS

調味料・ドレッシング・
タレ・その他

NINGS  & SAUCES

Easy Japanese food is even easier if you have a few go-to sauces made up ahead of time, that you can dip into whenever you're craving a Japanese meal. Or not – even if you're cooking everything from scratch, these sauces are a breeze to bash together.

DASHI

The Japanese food educator Akemi Yokoyama explains that there are two 'pillars' of flavour in Japanese cuisine. One is **kōji**, the mould used to ferment staple seasonings such as soy sauce, miso and sake. The other is **dashi**, the light broth made from seaweed and (usually) dried fish. Indeed, dashi provides so much of the underlying umami in Japanese food that it's almost unimaginable without it. In home kitchens in Japan it is typically made from dashi powder, a convenient and surprisingly delicious little cheat that I wholeheartedly endorse (just make sure you buy *kombu* dashi powder rather than *katsuo* dashi powder, as the latter contains fish). But it is also easily made from scratch – if you've ever made tea, you have basically gone through the same process as making dashi.

The traditional vegan dashi in Japan is simply made from kombu (dried kelp), sometimes with dried mushrooms as well. I've also included a recipe for a third type of dashi using extra seaweeds. Mostly they are interchangeable, but where I think one is better than the other, I have indicated so in each recipe.

VEGAN DASHI THREE WAYS

TOASTED KOMBU DASHI

MAKES ABOUT 450 ML (15 FL OZ/SCANT 2 CUPS)

Dashi made with *katsuobushi* has a distinct smoky-fishy aroma and while traditional kombu dashi is delicious in its own right, it doesn't have quite the same impact as a katsuo dashi. So how do you get that bold, smoky flavour into a vegan dashi? Well, where there's smoke there's fire, right? So, I figured I needed to commit a little kombu arson.

You may already be aware that nori is toasted before it's made into sushi, to deepen its flavour and make its texture more brittle. I wondered if kombu would benefit from the same treatment. To toast the kombu, I figured I'd use the thing in my kitchen most suited to toasting: the toaster. This turned out to be problematic. The toaster was too good at its job and toasted the kombu too rapidly, filling my kitchen with acrid seaweed smoke, and it made the kombu too brittle, so bits of it broke off and got stuck in the bottom of the toaster. Plus, the resulting dashi tasted weird, like I'd tried to make dashi out of the remnants of a beachside bonfire. So that didn't work, but I was not discouraged.

For my next trial, I toasted the kombu over an open flame on my hob, so that it browned lightly and charred in spots, developing a strong, nutty, almost mushroom-like aroma. Then I proceeded to make the dashi in the usual fashion, by simply soaking it for a while in hot water. Truthfully, it didn't replicate the smokiness I was looking for, but it did produce possibly the most flavourful kombu dashi I've ever tasted. It was exceptionally rich on the palate, almost sweet – a taste sometimes described by sensory scientists as 'mouth-filling'. It is really very good, if I do say so myself, and it's incredibly easy.

10 g (½ oz) kombu (a piece about 10 cm/4 in square)
500 ml (17 fl oz/2 cups) cold water

Using tongs, hold the kombu about 5 cm (2 in) above an open flame on the hob, turning it and moving it around often so it toasts evenly; it should have some burnt black bits in places, but not too many. The whole process should only take a few minutes. If you don't have a gas hob, you can do this under the grill (broiler), but watch it very carefully so the whole thing doesn't blister and burn.

Place the toasted kombu in a saucepan with the water and set over a low heat. Slowly bring the water to a very low simmer – you should just see a few little bubbles breaking the surface. Remove from the heat, then leave to infuse for at least 30 minutes (the longer the better). Pass through a sieve (fine-mesh strainer) and store in the refrigerator for up to 1 week.

PRO TIP If you want to make really good dashi, use soft water. It sounds pretentious, but it really does make a difference, so if your tap water is hard, get a bottle of distilled water or low-mineral mineral water like Volvic. Also, whatever you do, don't let any of them boil while you're infusing them! Kombu, in particular, loses a lot of flavour when it boils, so keep the heat low and watch your dashi carefully.

DIFFICULTY
0% difficult

VEGAN DASHI THREE WAYS
CONTINUED

MUSHROOM DASHI

MAKES ABOUT 350 ML (12 FL OZ/SCANT
1½ CUPS), PLUS THE REHYDRATED MUSHROOMS

Mushroom dashi has a gorgeously rich flavour and, as an added bonus, you can eat the mushrooms after they're rehydrated. The porcini are not traditional, and you don't have to use them, but I love the deep, earthy note they add.

10 g (½ oz) kombu (a piece about 10 cm/4 in square)
15 g (⅔ oz) dried shiitake mushrooms,
    or 10 g (½ oz) dried shiitake plus 5 g (⅛ oz)
    dried porcini mushrooms
500 ml (17 fl oz/2 cups) cold water

Place the kombu and dried mushrooms in a saucepan with the water and set over a low heat. Slowly bring the water to a very low simmer – you should just see a few little bubbles breaking the surface. Remove from the heat, then leave to infuse for at least 1 hour – it will take a while for the shiitake to fully hydrate and release their flavour into the dashi. Remove the mushrooms and squeeze them out like a sponge, then pass through a sieve (fine-mesh strainer) and store in the refrigerator for up to 1 week. The mushrooms will keep in the refrigerator for about 4 days.

TRIPLE SEAWEED DASHI

MAKES ABOUT 400 ML (13 FL OZ/GENEROUS
1½ CUPS), PLUS ENOUGH WAKAME FOR 4 BOWLS
OF MISO SOUP OR A SMALL SALAD

This dashi builds on the briny flavour of kombu with two other seaweeds, nori and wakame, for a complex, oceanic aroma and full-on umami. This is a great dashi to use in miso soup, which will also provide a use for the rehydrated wakame.

10 g (½ oz) kombu (a piece about 10 cm/4 in square)
1 sheet of nori
5 g (⅛ oz) dried wakame
500 ml (17 fl oz/2 cups) cold water

Place all the seaweeds in a saucepan with the water and set over a low heat. Slowly bring the water to a very low simmer – you should just see a few little bubbles breaking the surface. Remove from the heat, then leave to infuse for at least 30 minutes. Pass through a sieve (fine-mesh strainer) and store in the refrigerator for up to 1 week. Salvage the wakame for later use in a salad or soup; it will keep in the refrigerator for about 4 days.

VEGAN TSUYU
(FORTIFIED DASHI)

Tsuyu is essentially dashi that's been seasoned and usually concentrated to fortify its flavour. It's used as a dip, especially for noodles or tempura, but also as a liquid stock base that can be topped up with water for a flavourful broth. You can buy tsuyu in shops, but it usually contains *katsuobushi*, so it's verboten for vegans. And anyway, it's very easy to make yourself and it's a great way of prolonging the shelf life of dashi so you can have it on hand whenever you need it.

400 ml (13 fl oz/generous 1½ cups) dashi
    (any kind, pages 33–34)
6 tablespoons soy sauce
4 tablespoons mirin

Bring the dashi to the boil and let it reduce by about half. Remove from the heat and add the soy sauce and mirin. Leave to cool, then transfer to a jar and store in the refrigerator for up to 1 month.

Used in concentrated form as a dip, this will be enough for about 4 servings of tempura or 2 servings of cold noodles (add some grated/shredded daikon or radish to the tsuyu to help it cling more effectively as a dip). To use it as a broth, simply top it up with water (about 200 ml/7 fl oz/scant 1 cup should do) until it tastes like nicely seasoned dashi, then use it in a bowl of hot noodles or as a base for other dishes.

NOTE Daikon is a big white radish, often called mooli, which is the Urdu word for it. The flavour is like a cross between a radish and a turnip. In most cases, ordinary radishes will make a fine substitute.

DIFFICULTY
Tsuyu really think I'd include this recipe if it was at all difficult?

SWEET MISO SAUCE

This delicious and versatile sauce is known as *dengaku miso* in Japanese, and it adorns a wide range of traditional vegan delights, including grilled aubergine (eggplant), tofu, dumplings and simmered vegetables. It's great used as is, but it caramelises beautifully when cooked, so I like it best in dishes that are roasted or otherwise exposed to a strong, dry heat. It couldn't be simpler to make – everything just gets stirred together – and it lasts forever in the refrigerator, so this recipe is for a big batch (but feel free to scale the recipe down if you like).

300 g (10½ oz) miso (I like a blend of white and red miso for this, but if forced to choose I'd go with red)
6 tablespoons mirin
50–60 g (2 oz/scant ⅓ cup) sugar (any kind), to taste
3 tablespoons water or sake
1½ teaspoons vinegar (optional and not traditional, but I like it)

Stir everything together until no lumps of miso remain and the sugar has dissolved. Store in a jar in the refrigerator for up to 6 months.

DIFFICULTY
You will not believe how not difficult this is

SWEET SOY SAUCE

This is a basic sweetened, thickened soy sauce, similar to a classic teriyaki sauce, yakitori sauce or kabayaki 'eel sauce', which are all similar, but with minor variations in the ratios of their constituent parts. Like Sweet Miso Sauce (page 39), it's a great all-purpose 'Japanifier' to keep in the refrigerator and, also like sweet miso sauce, it benefits from a little bit of caramelisation. It's a fantastic, deep, palate-pleasing condiment to have on hand, almost indescribably delicious when stirred through mayonnaise or when spiked with a little hot chilli sauce.

It is also endlessly customisable – see below for how to adjust the flavour to your liking.

100 ml (3½ fl oz/scant ½ cup) soy sauce
15 g (½ oz/2 tablespoons) cornflour (cornstarch)
150 ml (5 fl oz/scant ⅔ cup) sake
3 tablespoons mirin
50 g (2 oz/¼ cup) light brown sugar

Stir a little bit of the soy sauce (3–4 tablespoons) into the cornflour to make a thin slurry. Combine the remaining soy sauce with the sake, mirin and sugar in a saucepan. Bring to a low boil, then simmer for a few minutes to cook off the alcohol in the sake. Whisk in the soy sauce-cornflour slurry and simmer for a few more minutes to thicken the sauce. Taste and adjust as necessary:

LESS SALTY	→ add more sake or mirin
LESS SWEET	→ add more soy sauce or sake
SWEETER	→ more sugar (duh)
SALTIER	→ add more soy sauce or a pinch of sea salt
MORE UMAMI	→ add some dashi or a little piece of kombu
RICHER	→ use tamari instead of regular soy sauce, or use dark brown sugar instead of light brown, or thicken with additional cornflour (cornstarch)
MORE COMPLEX	→ add a couple of smashed garlic cloves, some crushed black pepper, a bit of dried chilli and/or some grated (shredded) root ginger as the sauce simmers, then leave to infuse

DIFFICULTY
Teriyakifically not difficult

SEASONED VINEGAR

MAKES ABOUT 300 ML (10 FL OZ/1¼ CUPS)

Seasoned and sweetened rice vinegar turns up in all kinds of Japanese dishes, especially sushi, salads and pickles. Variations differ in the quantities of salt and sugar used, but you can make this one basic seasoning to use for all of them, with small additions to adjust the flavour in individual recipes. Or you can just buy the pre-bottled 'sushi vinegar' sold in Asian supermarkets – it's easy and delicious, so really it depends on what's easier for you: going to the shop, or just bashing this together at home.

250 ml (8½ fl oz/1 cup) rice vinegar
80 g (3 oz/⅓ cup) caster (superfine) or granulated (raw) sugar
1 tablespoon fine salt
1 small piece (about 5 cm/2 in square) kombu, or ½ teaspoon or so of kombu dashi powder

Combine everything in a small saucepan and bring to a very low simmer. Stir to dissolve the salt and sugar, then remove from the heat. If you're using kombu, leave to infuse for at least 20 minutes. Once cool, transfer to a jar. It'll keep at room temperature forever, and you can leave the kombu in there – it'll just get more and more umami as time goes on.

DIFFICULTY
Time to bust out the thesaurus to find the most extreme antonym to 'difficult'

'DEEP ROAST' SESAME DRESSING

MAKES 500 ML (17 FL OZ/2 CUPS)

Sesame dressing is truly wonderful stuff, addictively creamy and tangy, and rich with the irresistible nutty aroma of sesame. You can buy it in Asian supermarkets (and by all means do so, it's tasty and inexpensive), but it's also dead easy to make at home, with ordinary supermarket ingredients. This recipe really ramps up the roasty-toasty aroma by pan-frying the sesame paste to provide an incredible bittersweet, caramelised flavour.

100 g (3½ oz/scant ½ cup) tahini
100 g (3½ oz/¾ cup) sesame seeds
300 ml (10 fl oz/1¼ cups) soy milk
2 tablespoons sesame oil
90 ml (3 fl oz/6 tablespoons) vinegar
2 tablespoons caster (superfine) or granulated (raw) sugar
90 ml (3 fl oz/6 tablespoons) soy sauce
½ teaspoon salt
½ teaspoon dashi powder

Tip the tahini and sesame seeds into a frying pan (skillet), ideally non-stick, and set over a medium-high heat. Fry for about 10 minutes, stirring constantly, until it is noticeably more aromatic and darker in colour (it should go from camel-coloured to... let's say *taupe)*. Remove the tahini from the pan and leave to cool, then stir in the remaining ingredients until the sugar dissolves. Store in the refrigerator for 1 week (it will start to taste a bit stale after this; if you don't think you'll get through it quickly enough, the recipe is easily halved).

DIFFICULTY
Deliciously not difficult

VEGAN JAPANESE MAYO

When I made this mayo, I was struck by two things: 1) it's unbelievably easy, almost certainly the easiest mayo I've ever made, and 2) it's really really really delicious. Japanese mayo – specifically the brand Kewpie – is known for its rich flavour and smooth, creamy consistency, achieved by using only egg yolks rather than whole eggs, as well as other flavoursome seasonings such as malt vinegar and MSG. So I was surprised at how successful this was, using no eggs at all, and no MSG. It uses soy milk as an emulsifier, which becomes light and airy as the mayo is whipped, and it also contributes a vaguely tofu-esque flavour, which is not particularly authentic but still very amenable to Japanese dishes. It really is fantastic – if you've ever been daunted by making mayo, then this will do away with your dauntedness decidedly!

100 ml (3½ fl oz/scant ½ cup) unsweetened soy milk
1 tablespoon nutritional yeast flakes
2 tablespoons prepared mustard (Dijon is best, but any kind will do, except grain mustard)
½ teaspoon soy sauce
½ teaspoon salt
180 ml (6 fl oz/¾ cup) neutral, light vegetable oil (sunflower is good)
1 tablespoon vinegar

Combine everything (yes everything, even the oil) in a food processor or the container for a hand-held stick blender. Blend for a minute until everything comes together and thickens (you may need to scrape the sides of the bowl down once or twice). Alternatively, you can just whisk the hell out of everything in a bowl until it comes together. The soy proteins will form a foam within the mayo, and it will continue to aerate as you whisk or blend it, so keep whisking if you want this to be super light and airy – or stop if you want it to be more dense and creamy.

DIFFICULTY
Easier (and tastier) than most mayos I've known

PONZU

Ponzu isn't just one of the most lovely seasonings in Japanese cookery, it's one of the most lovely seasonings in the world. It's also fun to say. Ponzu ponzu ponzu. The marriage of lipsmacking citrus acidity with the all-round deliciousness of soy sauce is simply ingenious, and ingeniously simple.

200 ml (7 fl oz/scant 1 cup) soy sauce
juice of 2 lemons or 3–4 limes (or use a mix of both, about 3 tablespoons in total*)
20–30 g (¾–1 oz/1½–2½ tablespoons) caster (superfine) or granulated (raw) sugar (to taste)

Stir everything together until the sugar dissolves. Taste and add more sugar as needed (it shouldn't be sweet, but it shouldn't be overly sour either; add enough sugar just to take the edge off).

*Feel free to get creative with the citrus element here! If you can get yuzu juice, that's a fantastic (but expensive) option, or you can use orange or grapefruit – just remember the sauce should be sharp, so if you're using sweeter citrus, add some lemon or lime as well to make it nice and tart. Also, it's not that easy to come by, but I highly recommend bergamot in ponzu if you can get it – it has a deliciously lemongrassy/floral aroma that makes for a delightful sauce.

DIFFICULTY
Not difficult not difficult lemon not difficult

BATTER FOR BREADCRUMBING

This is bound to be the most boring recipe in this book, but what it lacks in excitement it makes up for in functionality. It's designed to mimic the viscosity and stickiness of eggs for breadcrumbing, but it's also a pretty good 'fish and chips'-type batter in its own right – although not as good, I suppose, as proper tempura batter (page 118).

100 g (3½ oz/¾ cup) plain (all-purpose) flour
25 g (¾ oz/scant ¼ cup) cornflour (cornstarch)
200 ml (7 fl oz/scant 1 cup) water

Stir together the plain flour and cornflour until well mixed. Add the water and stir until no lumps remain. Keep in the refrigerator for up to 4 days.

DIFFICULTY
Eggsquisitely not difficult

TONKATSU SAUCE

Tonkatsu sauce is a sweet-and-sour Japanese brown sauce, which is, of course, served with tonkatsu (fried pork cutlets), but it has become one of the defining flavours of modern Japanese cookery, along with its many variants and offshoots such as yakisoba sauce and okonomiyaki sauce. The flavour is similar to a mixture of Worcestershire sauce and HP, but with a richer, sweeter character. Some supermarkets now sell it – the brands you're most likely to find are Bulldog and Otafuku. Both are delicious (and vegan) and you should buy them if you can. Making tonkatsu sauce is easy, but in truth, the bottled versions are better. I know you're not really supposed to say that sort of thing in a cookbook, but it's true. But it's like ketchup – the one you make yourself will probably never be as good as Heinz. Sorry not sorry. #heinz4life #heyheinzpleasegivemesomemoney

However, one good thing about making your own tonkatsu sauce is that you can adjust the flavour however you like it – more vinegar to make it more acidic, more tamarind if you like it fruitier, or a bit more mustard if you like it with a kick. So feel free to play around with the quantities as you see fit!

This makes a lot of tonkatsu sauce, but it is delicious and easy to get through, and anyway it keeps for several months in the refrigerator.

2½ teaspoons tomato purée (paste)
½ teaspoon allspice
¼ teaspoon English mustard powder
¼ teaspoon garam masala or mild curry powder
1½ tablespoons Marmite (yeast extract)
150 g (5 oz/¾ cup) brown sugar
2 tablespoons mushroom ketchup
1½ tablespoons cider vinegar
150 ml (5 fl oz/scant ⅔ cup) ketchup
150 ml (5 fl oz/scant ⅔ cup) HP or similar brown sauce
4 tablespoons tamarind paste

Stir together the tomato purée, spices, Marmite and brown sugar to make a thick paste. Whisk in the mushroom ketchup, vinegar, ketchup, brown sauce and tamarind paste until smooth. Best made at least 1 hour before you need it, to let the sugar and spices dissolve properly. Store in a jar, or better yet a squeezy bottle, in the refrigerator for up to 6 months.

DIFFICULTY
Splendidly not difficult

JAPANESE CURRY ROUX
(AKA NOT KATSU SAUCE)

Things don't always go the way you hoped. I wanted to be an astronaut, but I was told I can't because I wear glasses. Also because I'm too fat, dumb and lazy. And while it's disappointing that I'll never go to space, luckily I had a solid plan B to fall back on: to be the world's most insufferable pedant on the subject of katsu curry.

Here's the deal: katsu curry isn't a type of curry. I mean, it is, in the sense that chicken curry is a type of curry: 'katsu' is the thing that goes in or on the curry, not the curry itself. *Katsu* is short for *katsuretto*, the Japanified word for cutlet – originally used to describe schnitzel-esque breaded and fried cuts of meat, but now used to describe anything breaded and fried, provided it is vaguely cutlet-shaped. And katsu in Japan is usually served with katsu sauce (a common truncation of tonkatsu [pork katsu] sauce), which is of course named after the katsu itself, and tastes more or less like HP blended with Worcestershire sauce and a few extra spoonfuls of sugar (see Tonkatsu Sauce recipe, page 47). Katsu sauce is essentially brown sauce – not curry sauce. Curry sauce in Japan is just called *karē,* even though many people here in the UK call Japanese curry sauce 'katsu sauce'.

I learned long ago to not be too precious about how Japanese words are (mis)used in the Anglosphere. I once challenged my mother on her pronunciation of sake as 'saki', and she responded by sending me a link to Merriam-Webster's entry for *sake*, which listed 'saki' as an accepted pronunciation. I was so livid I actually wrote an angry e-mail to the dictionary. They replied (!) that 'sake' when used by English speakers, as part of English dialogue, isn't a Japanese word – it's an English word borrowed from Japanese denoting a Japanese thing and, much like similar loan words such as Champagne, ski or sauna, the English 'sake' is pronounced differently to how it is in its original native speech. Fair enough.

But I'll be honest: the sake issue *still* irks me, and the 'katsu sauce' issue even more so – not just because it's wrong and weird, but because it often leads to confusion. At the restaurant, people often get annoyed when we serve them katsu sauce, when what they were expecting was curry sauce. Even though 'katsu sauce' is exactly what they asked for!

Maybe it's too late; maybe the English term 'katsu' already means 'Japanese curry', as seen in Greggs's 'katsu chicken bake' or innumerable jarred supermarket 'katsu' curry sauces. But I'm still fighting it; to me it is just as vexing as someone calling a calzone a 'pasty', or a tuna melt 'pizza'. So close, yet so very, very far.

Whatever you call it, this is one of the most delectable sauces in Japanese cuisine – essentially a smooth, spiced gravy rather than a 'proper' curry sauce, it's a Japanese soul food staple. Japanese curry is usually prepared from a pre-made roux, which is sold in little blocks that kind of resemble chocolate bars. These are a mix of fat, starch and concentrated flavourings that melt into boiling water, thickening magically into a luxurious sauce. So, this is a recipe for a similar kind of roux – you can keep it in the refrigerator or freezer to have Japanese curry at a moment's notice, by following the methods below.

DIFFICULTY

Not difficult in the slightest

JAPANESE CURRY ROUX
(AKA NOT KATSU SAUCE)

MAKES 200 G (7 OZ), ENOUGH FOR 4 SERVINGS

3 tablespoons coconut oil
3 tablespoons vegetable oil
1 small onion, finely diced
½ small, ripe banana, diced
1 tablespoon tomato purée (paste)
1 tablespoon peanut butter or similar nut butter
60 g (2 oz/scant ½ cup) plain (all-purpose) flour
2 tablespoons curry powder
2 tablespoons garam masala
2 tablespoons nutritional yeast (optional)

Heat the coconut and vegetable oils together in a saucepan over a medium heat, then add the onion and sauté until soft and slightly brown. Add the banana and continue to cook until the banana browns and starts to break apart. Add the tomato purée, peanut butter, flour, spices and yeast flakes (if using) and cook for another 5 minutes, stirring constantly, until the spices have softened and the fat has absorbed the flour. Transfer to a food processor or use a hand-held stick blender to purée the roux. Leave to cool, then divide into 50 g (2 oz/3 tablespoons) portions and transfer to the refrigerator, where it will keep for about a week, or to the freezer, where it will keep for several months.

To reconstitute and season the roux, use the following measurements:

CURRY SAUCE

(1 PORTION)
USE THIS FOR VEGETABLE CURRY RICE
OR KATSU CURRY

200 ml (7 fl oz/scant 1 cup) dashi (any kind, pages 33–34) or seasoned vegetable broth
50 g (2 oz/3 tablespoons) curry roux
1½ teaspoons soy sauce
1½ teaspoons ketchup
hot chilli sauce, to taste

Bring the broth to the boil and add the roux, soy sauce and ketchup. Whisk to break up the roux and cook for 5–10 minutes until the mixture thickens. Taste and adjust the flavour with chilli sauce, as needed.

CURRY SOUP BROTH

(1 PORTION)
USE THIS FOR CURRY UDON OR CURRY RAMEN

300 ml (10 fl oz/1¼ cups) dashi (any kind, pages 33–34) or vegetable broth
50 g (2 oz/3 tablespoons) curry roux
1–2 tablespoons soy sauce (to taste)
hot chilli sauce, to taste

Bring the broth to the boil and add the roux. Whisk to break up the roux and cook for 5–10 minutes until the mixture thickens. Add the soy sauce, then taste and adjust the flavour with more soy sauce and chilli sauce, as needed.

DIFFICULTY
Not difficult in the slightest

WAFU DRESSING
(SWEET ONION AND GINGER DRESSING)

MAKES ABOUT 350 ML (12 FL OZ/SCANT 1½ CUPS),
ENOUGH FOR AT LEAST 6 SALADS

This dressing, whose name means 'Japanese style', is perhaps the most ubiquitous salad dressing in Japan, and something everybody should have in their culinary repertoire because it's just so delicious (and so easy). When you read the ingredients, which include raw onions and ginger, it sounds as though it will be harsh and intense, but actually its flavour, while strong, is surprisingly mellow and balanced. This is a particularly good dressing to have on hand if you want to 'Japanify' a simple meal – it's great on a salad, of course, which can then be paired with rice, miso soup and another simple, small dish for a full Japanese dinner, but it also makes a great marinade, especially for grilled veggies.

¼ onion or ½ banana shallot
2 cm (¾ in) piece of fresh ginger root, peeled
100 ml (3½ fl oz/scant ½ cup) soy sauce
100 ml (3½ fl oz/scant ½ cup) mirin
100 ml (3½ fl oz/scant ½ cup) rice vinegar
1 tablespoon sesame oil
1 tablespoon sesame seeds

Finely grate the onion and ginger and combine with all the other ingredients. Stir to combine and, ideally, let it sit for 30 minutes or so for all the flavours to come together. Alternatively, bung everything in a food processor and whizz it up until the onion and ginger are broken down. Store in a jar in the refrigerator for up to a month (it won't go off, but the flavours will start to fade).

DIFFICULTY

Not at all difficult

SMALL DISH

SNACKS,

一品料理

& SIDES

These small, simple dishes can be mixed and matched with each other, or served with a pan of rice to make a full Japanese meal – or not! Many of them are excellent side dishes for all sorts of meals, not just Japanese, or lovely little snacks on their own.

PICKLES!

MAKES ENOUGH TO FILL A LARGE (1 LITRE/34 FL OZ) JAR

If you're vegan, you're probably accustomed to some level of misguided pity: 'Oh you're vegan? How saaaaaad, you can't have [circle one] bacon/roast chicken/steak/fermented shark/cheese.' And maybe that is sad, I don't know. But they're evidently forgetting that you can still have PICKLES, which are seriously one of the world's most wonderful foods – invigoratingly tart and flavoursome, a quintessential side dish to all kinds of meals, or just a fantastic snack in their own right. And, luckily, Japan is a pickle paradise – the recipes that follow are just the tip of the fermented iceberg.

KIMCHI / PICKLED CABBAGE

Kimchi is not Japanese, it's Korean. So what's it doing in a Japanese cookbook, you ask? Well, it's been enthusiastically adopted in Japan, finding a home in Japanified Korean recipes like Kimchi Miso Hotpot (page 123) and Kimchi and Tofu Gyoza (page 103). There is a traditional Japanese equivalent, which forgoes the spice for a cleaner, pure cabbage flavour accented by citrus. This is an altogether more delicate, more 'Japanese' preparation, but the method is the same.

KIMCHI

900 g (2 lb) Chinese cabbage (this is usually about 1 whole head of cabbage, but you should still weigh it), cut into big chunks
20 g (¾ oz/4 teaspoons) salt
25 g chilli powder/flakes (+10,000,000 authenticity points for using Korean chilli, -1,000 for using some other chilli)
3–4 spring onions (scallions), coarsely chopped
20 g (¾ oz) fresh root ginger, peeled and finely grated (shredded)
1 sheet of nori, cut into tiny pieces, or 1 tablespoon nori flakes
6 garlic cloves, minced (ground)

JAPANESE PICKLED CABBAGE

900 g (2 lb) Chinese cabbage (this is usually about 1 whole head of cabbage, but you should still weigh it), cut into big chunks
20g (¾ oz/4 teaspoons) salt
zest of 1 lemon
5 cm (2 in) square piece of kombu, soaked in water until soft, then finely grated (shredded)

Combine all the ingredients and mix well. Leave for 20–30 minutes for the salt to work on the cabbage, drawing out its moisture. Massage the cabbage and squeeze it, getting as much salty cabbage juice out as possible. Leave to sit for another 20–30 minutes and repeat.

Pack everything into a jar really tightly and pour over any remaining cabbage juice. Push the cabbage down into the jar with all your might, so the juice rises above the surface. If there's not enough liquid, leave it for another 30 minutes or so and then come back and continue to pack it down; the cabbage needs to be fully submerged in the brine or it could go mouldy. Once your cabbage is satisfactorily covered in a good 5 mm (¼ in) of brine, cover the jar – I just screw the cap on so it's still loose, but you can also use a cloth bound with a rubber band or string.*

Leave to ferment at room temperature for about 1 week, then taste it – when it's nice and sour, it's good to go. (This could take longer if your house runs a bit cold, or if you live under the stairs like Harry Potter.)

When your kimchi is sour enough to your liking, seal the jar and transfer to the refrigerator, where it will keep more or less forever (honestly – I've had homemade kimchi and sauerkraut for years).

WARNING: NEVER seal a jar of kimchi or any other ferment tightly; the gas produced by fermentation builds up within the jar and could cause it to explode.

DIFFICULTY
It is difficult explaining to your other half why the kitchen smells of cabbage farts, but less so when you present them with delicious homemade kimchi

CITRUS-PICKLED RADISHES

Pickled radishes smell funny (Chef: 'I think these pickled radishes have gone off'. Me: 'No, that's just how they smell'.), but they taste awesome – crisp and crunchy and sour and refreshing. And they look cool, too – the pink pigment from the skins leaches into the brine, and then back into the rads themselves, turning them a striking fluorescent fuschia colour. The citrus in the brine adds a lovely freshness, and this can be used for pretty much any other crunchy veg as well – it's especially nice with carrots.

3 tablespoons yuzu juice (or lime juice, if you can't get yuzu)
juice of 1 lemon (about 25 ml/1½ tablespoons)
3 tablespoons vinegar
3 tablespoons sake
1 teaspoon salt
1½ tablespoons caster (superfine) sugar
150 g (5 oz) radishes, halved

Stir together everything except the radishes until the salt and sugar dissolve. Pack the radishes into a jar and pour over the brine (don't worry if the radishes aren't fully submerged or if they float – they'll absorb the brine and pickle nicely). They'll be ready to eat the next day, but will be better after 2 or 3 days. Keep in the refrigerator for up to 2 months.

DIFFICULTY
Radishiously not difficult

SHIITAKE PICKLED IN SOY SAUCE

MAKES ENOUGH TO FILL A SMALL (200 ML/7 FL OZ) JAR

These intensely meaty morsels are a great way to add flavour to dishes, of course, but they're also a great way of getting a second use out of dried shiitake if you've used them to make Mushroom Dashi (page 34). This recipe doesn't make very much, but their flavour is very strong, so a little of them go a long way.

4–5 dried shiitake (or however many you have from making Mushroom Dashi, page 34), rehydrated, destemmed and thinly sliced
1 dried red chilli, cut in half, or a little pinch of chilli flakes (optional)
4 tablespoons soy sauce
2 tablespoons mirin
1 tablespoon rice vinegar

Pack the sliced mushrooms and the chilli into a little jar and pour over the soy sauce, mirin and vinegar. Leave to pickle for at least 2 hours, but they'll be better if you leave them for a few days. Keep in the refrigerator for up to 6 months.

DIFFICULTY
Magically not difficult

RED PICKLED GINGER

There are two main types of pickled ginger in Japan: there's gari, the thinly-sliced, sweet stuff that comes with sushi, and there's beni shōga, the alarmingly red, julienned version that adorns many soul food dishes like ramen, okonomiyaki and yakisoba. This recipe is for the latter, because it's less likely to be found on supermarket shelves – but if you can buy it, by all means do. You can also use sushi ginger in its place, but for me the flavour is too sweet – add a bit of vinegar to the sushi vinegar brine if you're planning to use it as a topping.

By the way, in Japan this is made with 'young' ginger, which you can sometimes get at Asian supermarkets, identifiable by its smooth, yellow skin and reddish tips. This ginger is fresh and sweet and doesn't need to be peeled, so if you come across it, by all means stock up.

200 g (7 oz) fresh root ginger, peeled
1½ tablespoons salt
100 ml (3½ fl oz/scant ½ cup) rice vinegar plus
    100 ml (3½ fl oz/scant ½ cup) pickled beetroot
    (beet) brine, or 150 ml (5 fl oz/scant ⅔ cup) rice
    vinegar plus 3 tablespoons beetroot juice (in
    Japan they use pink plum vinegar, called umezu,
    for this – if you can find it, use it)
1 tablespoon caster (superfine) sugar

Julienne the ginger to matchstick size, about 3 mm (⅛ in) thick. Massage in ½ tablespoon of the salt and leave to sit for about 30 minutes.

Meanwhile, preheat the oven to its lowest setting (or, if you have a dehydrator, get it out of the closet and switch it on to medium heat: 60–65°C/140–150°F).

Squeeze the ginger of all its juice and discard the liquid. Lay the ginger slices in an even layer on a non-stick baking sheet and transfer to the oven or dehydrator. Leave to dry out for about 2 hours (this will help it absorb the brine and maintain a crunchy texture).

Transfer the ginger to a jar, stir together the vinegar and beet brine/juice with the sugar and remaining 1 tablespoon of salt until the sugar dissolves. Pour over the ginger and leave to pickle for at least 1 day. Keep in the refrigerator for up to a year.

DIFFICULTY
Peeling the ginger is tedious but I wouldn't call it difficult

PIMP YOUR EDAMAME

A SNACK FOR 2, OR 1 IF YOU'RE GREEDY LIKE ME

Edamame is always delightful – the hands-on, peel-and-eat quality of it somehow makes it more fun and addictive – but it's also a blank slate in terms of flavour. Usually it's seasoned with nothing more than salt, which is nice, but it's also a little boring, don't you think? I mean, at the end of the day you're munching on salted beans. Honestly, it sounds like something a cartoon hobo would eat. But you can easily turn your edamame from lugubrious legumes into SUPER SOY POWER PODS with any of these seasoning ideas.

TRIPLE SESAME EDAMAME

Three forms of sesame – white, black and oil – double down on edamame's subtle nuttiness, making these exceptionally more-ish.

1 tablespoon black sesame seeds,
   roasted and crushed
1 tablespoon white sesame seeds,
   roasted and crushed
a few pinches of salt
250 g (9 oz) frozen edamame
1 teaspoon sesame oil

Stir together the sesame seeds and salt. Boil the edamame from frozen until tender, about 2–3 minutes, then drain. Immediately toss with the sesame seed-salt mixture and the sesame oil.

CHILLI PONZU EDAMAME

If you have a short attention span, this is the edamame for you. They are really spicy, so at the very least they're not going to be boring. Avoid if you are prone to heartburn!

a few splashes of very hot chilli sauce
juice of ½ lime
1 tablespoon soy sauce
2 teaspoons sesame seeds
1 teaspoon shichimi or similar chilli powder
250 g (9 oz) frozen edamame

Have all the seasonings measured and ready. Boil the edamame from frozen until tender, about 2–3 minutes, then drain. Immediately toss with all of the seasonings.

CHEESE AND ONION EDAMAME

Edamame has a mindlessly addictive quality that reminds me of crisps (chips), which are what inspired this recipe for 'cheese-and-onion'-flavoured edamame, which is surprisingly easy and insanely tasty.

1 tablespoon nutritional yeast flakes
½ teaspoon onion granules
¼ teaspoon salt
250 g (9 oz) frozen edamame
1 teaspoon olive oil
½ teaspoon vinegar

Crush the nutritional yeast into a powder, then mix together with the onion granules and salt. Boil the edamame from frozen until tender, about 2–3 minutes, then drain. Immediately toss with all of the seasonings. Leave to sit for a few minutes before tucking in; the steam from the edamame will release more onion aroma.

DIFFICULTY
So not difficult that if these are beyond your grasp as a cook,
you should probably find a new hobby

ONIGIRI / YAKI-ONIGIRI
(RICE BALLS / GRILLED RICE BALLS)

MAKES 6

Onigiri is commonly translated as 'rice balls', but actually they're more commonly little rice triangles. At their most basic, they're just rice in a convenient hand-held format, but they can also be stuffed with all kinds of flavourful fillings and/or grilled with a salty condiment, giving them exquisitely crisp, rice cracker-like crusts. If you plan to make a lot of onigiri (a plan I wholeheartedly endorse), you may want to buy an onigiri mould at a Japanese supermarket or online – they make the process much faster and easier. Having said that, I quite like shaping onigiri by hand, even though I'm not very good at it; the repetitive movements are somewhat meditative.

300 g (10½ oz/1½ cups) rice (uncooked weight)
a few pinches of sea salt
fillings of your choosing (see opposite; optional)
1 sheet of nori, cut into 6 rectangles

YAKI-ONIGIRI

1 tablespoon sesame oil
4 tablespoons Sweet Miso Sauce (page 39)
a little bit of oil, for greasing
seame seeds, to garnish
1 sheet of nori, cut into 6 rectangles

To make onigiri, cook the rice according to the instructions on page 26, then tip it out onto a plate to cool. When it's cool enough to handle, wet your hands to keep the rice from sticking and grab a big handful of rice. Compress the rice into a ball, using the joint between your thumb and index finger on your dominant hand to press the ball into a triangular shape, while using your other hand to grip the ball and flatten it into a kind of patty. Or just manipulate it into a puck shape – this is also an acceptable style of onigiri. Finished onigiri can be kept in the refrigerator, covered, for up to 4 days, but if you're not eating them fresh, give them at least 30 minutes to come up to room temperature before eating. Wrap each onigiri in a rectangle of nori just before eating.

If you're adding fillings, before you start to compress the rice, flatten it out in your hand a bit. Add about 1 heaped tablespoonful of filling to the middle of the rice, then fold the rice up around it before shaping as above. Fillings can be just about anything, but they should be finely chopped and strongly flavoured: Shiitake Pickled in Soy Sauce (page 59), Kimchi (page 56), a little bit of leftover Sichuan-Style Hot and Numbing Tofu (page 124), or any kind of shop-bought Japanese pickles are good options. Also, instead of fillings, you can just work seasonings into the rice itself – finely chopped pickles work here as well, or you can go for the classic goma-wakame: toasted white sesame seeds and chopped-up, rehydrated wakame seaweed.

If you're making yaki-onigiri, stir together the sesame oil and sweet miso sauce. Lay the onigiri onto a lightly oiled baking sheet or rack and brush the sauce over one side. Place under a hot grill (broiler), on the second-highest oven rack, until the sauce begins to char. Turn each onigiri over and repeat. Garnish with sesame seeds. Wrap each yaki-onigiri in nori before eating.

DIFFICULTY
It is a little bit difficult making onigiri into nice equilateral triangles;
luckily, you don't really have to do that, so ultimately this is not difficult

KALE WITH CRUSHED SESAME

(KĒRU NO GOMA-AE)

SERVES 4

I like all vegetables done goma-ae-style (coated in crushed sesame), but I especially like it with kale, because it makes kale less horrid. Kale is also the perfect vehicle for this preparation, because the intricate fractals of its leaves provide a lot of surface area and little nooks for the sesame seeds to get stuck in. In other words, it is an ideal sesame seed delivery device. This is a super-simple version of goma-ae using just sesame seeds and seasonings, but you can also make it with 'Deep Roast' Sesame Dressing (page 42) for a rich, creamy, slightly more involved (but still dead easy) version.

salt
200–300 g (7–10½ oz) kale, tough stalks removed and discarded
2 tablespoons toasted sesame seeds, crushed to the consistency of coarse sand (don't cheat and use untoasted sesame seeds because it will taste weird that way, and it will make you sad)
1 tablespoon soy sauce
1 tablespoon mirin
¼ teaspoon sesame oil

Bring a pan of water to the boil and add enough salt to make it taste seawater-salty. Add the kale and boil for just a few minutes, until tender but still with some bite. Drain very well, then toss with the sesame seeds, soy sauce, mirin and sesame oil.

This can also be enjoyed cold (it works well in a bento) – keep in the refrigerator for up to 4 days.

DIFFICULTY
Easily not difficult

SWEET POTATO WITH TRUFFLED PONZU

SERVES 4

In Japan, baked sweet potatoes are sold out of the backs of little trucks, cooked and kept warm on a bed of hot stones. They have a honey-sweet aroma I find irresistible, and Japanese sweet potatoes in particular are so sweet and lovely that they are sold completely unadorned and unseasoned. And that's nice, but I can't put that in a recipe book ('Ingredients: sweet potatoes. Method: bake sweet potatoes. The end.') So this is a marginally more complex preparation that matches the potatoes' sweetness with the acidity of ponzu, and accents its earthiness with a tiny bit of truffle (which is totally optional, by the way).

4 medium-sized sweet potatoes (about 600 g/ 1 lb 5 oz), ideally purple or white, washed
1 tablespoon sesame oil
4 tablespoons Ponzu (page 44)
a few drops of truffle oil, or – if you are very fancy – 5 g (¼ oz) fresh black truffle, finely grated (shredded)
a few pinches of black and white sesame seeds (or just white if you don't have black)

Preheat the oven to 220°C (430°F/Gas 9).

Brush each sweet potato with sesame oil, then wrap in kitchen foil and place on a baking sheet. Bake for 30–50 minutes, until they're soft throughout (I always use a chopstick to test whether they're done or not – it should easily pierce the potato and slip straight through). Remove from the oven and leave to cool slightly.

Meanwhile, stir together the ponzu, truffle oil or grated truffle, and any remaining sesame oil left over from brushing. Unwrap the potatoes, slice them down the middle, and drizzle over the ponzu mixture. Garnish with sesame seeds.

DIFFICULTY
Not difficult!!!!!!!

SQUASH BRAISED IN DASHI WITH MIRIN AND GINGER

SERVES 4

This is one of my all-time favourite ways of preparing humble gourds, a true classic of Japanese home cooking that heightens the sweetness of squash with a generous dose of mirin. You can use just about any squash you like, but it's best with dense, sweet varieties, especially kabocha – a Japanese cultivar of pumpkin with orange flesh and tender green skin, sometimes sold as 'Delica pumpkins'.

Also, can we take a moment to appreciate the words 'squash' and 'pumpkin', two of the silliest, most joyous words in the English language.

1 large-ish or 2 small-ish squashes or pumpkins – kabocha (Delica) is ideal, but butternut, acorn, red kuri, delicata and crown prince are also tasty
500 ml (17 fl oz/2 cups) Kombu or Mushroom Dashi (pages 33–34)
2 cm (¾ in) piece of fresh root ginger, peeled and finely shredded
4 tablespoons mirin
2 tablespoons soy sauce
1 tablespoon sake
water, as needed

If you're using a variety of squash with tough, inedible skin, peel it. If not, go ahead and leave it on. Cut the squash into wedges no thicker than 5 cm (2 in) at their widest end and place in a large saucepan.

Stir together the dashi, half of the grated ginger, mirin, soy sauce and sake. Pour the dashi mixture into the pan and add just enough water to barely cover the squash. Place a cartouche (a circle of baking parchment) over the squash, or a lid that fits just inside the pan so that it rests directly on top of the squash. Bring to the boil, then reduce to a high simmer and cook for about 10–15 minutes, until the squash is soft enough to cut with a spoon. If you can, this is better prepared ahead of time and left to sit for a while – the squash will absorb more dashi this way. It's good at room temperature, too, but feel free to reheat it if it's too cold for your liking.

Serve the squash with some of the dashi poured over, and garnish with the remaining grated ginger.

DIFFICULTY
Really not difficult

TERIYAKI-ROASTED CARROTS
(AKA BEST CARROTS EVER)

SERVES 4

Most Japanese domestic kitchens don't have ovens (except perhaps a toaster oven), which means there isn't much roasting done there. So this recipe can't really be called authentic, but do you know what it can be called? REALLY F$%KING DELICIOUS. In fact, this might be my favourite way to cook carrots *ever*. Roasting them on a high heat gives the carrots a delectable fudgy consistency, and the sweet-and-salty flavour of caramelised teriyaki sauce makes them sticky and unctuous.

500–600 g (1 lb 2 oz–1 lb 5 oz) carrots (I like chantenay carrots for this because I am lazy and they require no prep, but any carrots will do)
2 tablespoons oil, plus a little extra for greasing
8 tablespoons Sweet Soy Sauce (page 40)
zest of ½ orange or lemon

If you're using little carrots like chantenay, preheat the oven to 220ºC (430°F/Gas 9). If you're using big carrots, preheat it to 200ºC (400°F/Gas 7). The sweet soy sauce has a tendency to stick to roasting pans, so if you haven't got a non-stick one, it's a good idea to line the pan with baking parchment.

Toss the carrots in the oil, ensuring they are evenly coated, then use a little more to rub onto the roasting pan or parchment. Spread the carrots out in the pan and roast for 20 minutes (if they're small) or 30 (if they're big). Check to see if they're tender throughout with a fork or chopstick – if they're still too hard, keep roasting them in 5-minute increments until they're soft.

Pour over 6 tablespoons of the sweet soy and add the citrus zest, and toss so that all the carrots are evenly coated. Place back in the oven for 5–10 minutes, checking them often to ensure they aren't burning. The carrots are done when the sauce has reduced to a very thick, dark, sticky glaze that clings to the carrots.

Remove from the oven, add the remaining 2 tablespoons of sweet soy sauce, and toss. Leave to cool slightly before serving.

DIFFICULTY
Infinitely not difficult

TOFU PATTIES
(GANMODOKI)

These little pucks of protein turn up in all sorts of Japanese meals, but for some reason I always associate them with lunch. Some people translate them as tofu 'burgers', and while as a burger purist I find this irksome, the description is apt: they're dense and filling, with plenty of shiitake mushrooms for meaty texture and flavour. They're also good cold, so they're a perfect choice for a vegan bento (page 170). They're also great as a topping for noodles or hotpots.

5 dried shiitake mushrooms, rehydrated in hot water, saving the rehydrating liquid, or you can just make Mushroom Dashi (page 34) and save the mushrooms
2 teaspoons oil
1 teaspoon sesame oil
½ onion, finely chopped
2 garlic cloves, finely grated
2 cm (¾ in) chunk of fresh root ginger, peeled and finely grated (shredded)
1 block (400 g/14 oz) firm (cotton) tofu
1 small carrot, peeled and grated (shredded)
50 g (2 oz/generous 1 cup) panko breadcrumbs, or perhaps a little more
2 spring onions (scallions), finely sliced
1 tablespoon white sesame seeds, or a mixture of white and black
big pinch each of salt and white pepper
oil, for shallow-frying (at least 2 tablespoons)

SAUCE (OPTIONAL)
4 tablespoons ketchup
2 tablespoons Mushroom Dashi (page 34) or the mushroom rehydrating liquid (see above)
2 tablespoons soy sauce

Drain the mushrooms, remove their stems and cut them into fine dice.

Heat the oils in a small pan and sauté the onion, garlic and ginger for 5 minutes or so, until the onions soften.

In a bowl, break up the tofu into small crumbles with your hand or a fork. Add the mushrooms, the fried onion mixture, carrot, panko, spring onions, sesame seeds, salt and white pepper and mix well, mashing the tofu into a kind of paste. Leave for 5 minutes or so for the panko to absorb the liquid in the mixture – it should form a sort of thick, moist, dough-like consistency. If the mixture is too wet, add a bit more panko. Form this mixture into 12 small patties, about 7 cm (3 in) across and 1.5–2 cm (¾ in) thick.

Pour a generous layer of oil into a frying pan (skillet) and place over a high heat. Fry the patties until deep brown on each side, then remove (you will have to do this in batches – if you're eating these hot and fresh, keep warm on a baking sheet in a low oven).

To make the sauce, simply stir everything together until smooth. You can also use Sweet Soy Sauce (page 40), Sweet Miso Sauce (page 39) or Tonkatsu Sauce (page 47) with these.

Serve the sauce on the side, or brush the sauce onto one side of each patty and grill (broil) on high for a few minutes until the glaze bubbles and caramelises and fuses with the patties.

DIFFICULTY
Not difficult TO THE MAX

JAPANESE MUSHROOM PARCELS WITH GARLIC AND SOY SAUCE

SERVES 2 AS A SIDE OR 1 AS A MAIN

I always associate this preparation, or simple variations thereof, with izakaya – the wonderful Japanese drinkeries-cum-eateries where the food is highly varied but always conducive to drinking loads of good sake or beer – typically salty, snacky, shareable, crowd-pleasing dishes with bold but not over-the-top flavours. This is exactly that kind of dish, mushrooms simply steamed in a foil parcel with plenty of garlic and soy sauce – tearing open the foil is like opening a present on a particularly garlicky Christmas morning. It's lovely on its own but I would strongly recommend enjoying this with sake – nothing too fancy, as the earthier flavours of cheaper sake are perfect for this mushroomy garlic umami funkbomb.

200 g (7 oz) Japanese mushrooms (such as enoki, shimeji (beech), shiitake and eringi (king oyster) – often supermarkets sell an 'exotic' mushroom pack containing a few of each of these, which are perfect)
2 tablespoons soy sauce
1½ teaspoons sake
1½ teaspoons olive oil
3–4 garlic cloves, crushed and thinly sliced
a few grinds of black pepper
a few sprigs of flat-leaf parsley, finely chopped
You will also need some sturdy kitchen foil

Preheat the oven to 220°C (430°F/Gas 9). Prepare the mushrooms: for enoki or shimeji, cut off their bottoms and break up any large clusters; for shiitake, simply remove the stems; for eringi, cut them into roughly bite-size pieces.

Stir together the soy sauce, sake, olive oil, sliced garlic, black pepper and parsley. Toss the prepared mushrooms with the soy sauce mixture.

Set a wide piece of kitchen foil (about 40 cm/ 16 in long) into a shallow bowl or dish, and place the mushrooms and the sauce into the middle of the foil. Gather up the sides of the foil to cover the mushrooms, crimping them together to form a tight seal. Place the parcel on a baking sheet and bake for 20 minutes.

Transfer the parcel to a plate, taking care not to tear the foil. Serve with the parcel closed and open it at the table.

DIFFICULTY
The only cult I'd join is the Not Diffi Cult, and this recipe would be our Kool-Aid

SWEET MISO-ROASTED BEETROOT

SERVES 2

Beetroots (beets) are seldom seen in Japan, which is kind of a shame because their earthy-sweet flavour works well with so many Japanese seasonings. Miso in particular is a perfect partner, adding a similar kind of salty-funky-fruity flavour you get from fresh cheeses, but of course it's totally vegan. These garnet-fleshed flavour nuggets are great on their own, hot from the oven, but they can also be enjoyed cold and worked through a salad for a light yet substantial lunch.

400–500 g (14 oz–1 lb 2 oz) raw beetroot (beets), washed and peeled (if they have stems you can leave them on if you like, just make sure they're free from any dirt or grit)
2 tablespoons oil
a small handful of pecans or walnuts (optional)
6 tablespoons Sweet Miso Sauce (page 39)
1 tablespoon tahini
1 tablespoon maple syrup or brown sugar
¼ teaspoon sesame oil

Preheat the oven to 180ºC (350°F/Gas 6).

If the beetroot are smaller than a ping pong ball, leave them whole; if they're bigger, cut them in half; and if they're enormous, cut them into quarters. Toss the prepared beetroot with the oil and lay out in a single layer in a roasting pan. Roast for 40 minutes, tossing them once or twice during this time.

Meanwhile, spread the nuts (if using) over a baking sheet and place in the oven for 10 minutes to toast. Leave to cool and then coarsely chop.

After 40 minutes the beetroot should be fork-tender; if not, let them roast for a while longer, checking them every 5–10 minutes. When the beetroot are soft enough for your liking, increase the oven temperature to 220ºC (430°F/Gas 9), and toss the beetroot with the sweet miso sauce, tahini, maple syrup/brown sugar and sesame oil. Place them back in the oven and roast for another 5–10 minutes until the miso sauce has caramelised slightly.

Garnish with the nuts, if using.

DIFFICULTY
The non-difficulty of this recipe is simply unbeetable

GRILLED SWEETCORN WITH PONZU, SHICHIMI AND BLACK SESAME

SERVES 4

I'm not usually a stickler for seasonality, but sweetcorn is just one of those things, like peaches, strawberries and mince pies, that simply has to be eaten in the correct season. Most of the year it is categorically not worth eating, all starchy and bland, but come September when the season is at its peak, you just can't beat it – kernels plump and firm and bursting with juicy-sweet flavour. Really good corn doesn't need much to make it delicious and, in fact, it is very nice just brushed with soy sauce. But I am also a huge fan of *elotes*, the Mexican preparation of sweetcorn with chilli, lime and cheese. This is a Japanese approximation of those flavours, with tangy ponzu, spicy shichimi and rich black sesame.

4 ears of corn – get good-quality, in-season corn still in its husk (or not, whatevs, this will still be tasty)
2 teaspoons sesame oil
4 tablespoons Ponzu (page 44)
4 tablespoons black sesame seeds, crushed to a coarse powder
1 teaspoon shichimi
1 teaspoon sea salt

Preheat the grill (broiler) to high.

Peel the corn and remove its silk, then blanch in boiling water for 5 minutes. Drain and leave to dry for a few minutes.

Transfer the corn to a baking sheet and brush with the sesame oil and ponzu. Place the corn under the grill and cook for 10 minutes or so, turning frequently so that the corn browns evenly on all sides (you can also do this on the barbecue – if you do, apply the oil and ponzu after grilling or it will all just drip onto the coals and you'll lose the flavour).

Stir together the black sesame, shichimi and salt until evenly mixed, and sprinkle this over the grilled corn, spreading it with your hands to ensure it is evenly coated.

DIFFICULTY
I'm struggling to come up with new ways of saying 'not difficult' that aren't too corny

CRISPY FRIED AUBERGINE WITH SPICY MISO SAUCE

This is essentially the flavours of the classic *nasu dengaku* – sweet miso-glazed aubergine (eggplant) – spiked with a bit of chilli and translated into an addictive, snacky format. I think I like them especially because they remind me so much of me – with a hardened outer shell that's easily broken to reveal a soft and squishy middle.

Aonori are green nori seaweed flakes, typically used as a garnish. If you can't get them you can leave them out of most recipes and it won't be a disaster, but you can also blitz up a sheet of sushi nori in a spice grinder, or snip it into little shreds with scissors, to get a similar effect.

6 tablespoons Sweet Miso Sauce (page 39)
juice of ¼ lemon
hot chilli sauce, to taste
1 aubergine (eggplant)
80 g (3 oz/scant ⅔ cup) plain (all-purpose) flour
2 eggs' worth of vegan egg replacer or ½ x recipe
    quantity of Batter for Breadcrumbing (page 46)
about 100 g (3½ oz/2⅓ cups) panko breadcrumbs
oil, for deep-frying (about 1 litre/34 fl oz/4 cups)
pinch of salt
a few pinches of aonori (optional)

Stir together the sweet miso sauce, lemon juice and chilli sauce; taste and add more chilli sauce until it's nice and hot.

Cut the aubergine into little nuggets, no larger than 2 cm (¾ in) across at their thickest. Dredge the aubergine chunks in flour, and then the egg replacer or batter, and then the panko, ensuring they are evenly coated.

Pour the oil into a very deep, wide saucepan, to come no higher than halfway up the sides and heat to 180°C (350°F). Carefully lower the breadcrumbed aubergine into the hot oil – you will probably need to do this in a couple of batches unless you're using a very wide pan (if there's too much in the oil it will cause the temperature to drop and the finished product may end up soft and oily). Fry for 8–10 minutes until the breadcrumbs are a deep golden brown, then remove with a slotted spoon and drain well on paper towels.

Season with a little bit of salt and aonori, and serve with the spicy miso sauce either drizzled over the top, or on the side for dipping.

DIFFICULTY
So very not difficult

PROPER MISO SOUP

There's an old saying that pizza is like sex: even when it's bad, it's still pretty good. I hate this saying because it's so painfully obvious that whoever came up with it has never had truly bad pizza or sex, both of which can be horrendous. But the sentiment is true of miso soup: even instant powdered miso soup is pretty tasty, adequately delivering a certain hot, salty, briny MSG hit. But making really good miso soup is nearly as easy as making ordinary miso soup, so you may as well do it properly. It takes only a tiny bit of effort to add extra texture, flavour and general heartiness to the always-delicious base of miso stirred into hot dashi.

4 tablespoons miso (use a good-quality aged red miso if you can)
600 ml (20 fl oz/2½ cups) dashi (any dashi is fine, including instant dashi; I like the Triple Seaweed, page 34, for this)
5 mm (¼ in) slice of fresh root ginger (unpeeled)
¼ leek, finely sliced
2 tablespoons dried wakame
2 shiitake mushrooms, destemmed and sliced (rehydrated dried mushrooms are ideal)
8 mangetout (snow peas) or snap peas
½ block (200 g/7 oz) firm silken tofu, cut into 1 cm (½ in) cubes
a few pinches of white sesame seeds

Combine the dashi and ginger and bring to the boil. Add the leek, wakame and shiitake to the pan, reduce the soup to a simmer and cook for a few minutes, until the leeks soften and the wakame plumps up. Add the mangetout/snap peas and cook for another minute, retaining their colour and texture. Fish out the ginger from the soup and discard. Remove from heat and whisk in the miso.

Divide the tofu among deep bowls and ladle over the soup and veg. Garnish with sesame seeds.

DIFFICULTY
Minimally more difficult than miso soup from a packet, but maximally more satisfying

CUCUMBER AND WAKAME
WITH SEASONED VINEGAR
(SUNOMONO)

SERVES 4

This ubiquitous side dish pairs the refreshing crunch of cucumber with the spinachy tenderness of wakame, seasoned with a sweet, salty vinegar dressing that makes it kind of a salad and kind of a pickle. Its flavour has an oceanic freshness that calls to mind oysters, but it's subtle enough to work alongside all kinds of different dishes. The dish also improves with time – the cucumber absorbs the vinegar and salt, giving it a firm crunch and mouthwatering gherkinesque acidity.

2 heaped tablespoons dried wakame
1 cucumber, cut in half lengthwise
big pinch of salt
15 g (⅔ oz) fresh root ginger, peeled and
    finely grated (shredded)
zest of 1 lime (optional)
6 tablespoons Seasoned Vinegar (page 41)

Cover the wakame in cold water and leave for about 30 minutes to rehydrate, then drain well, squeezing it to get out any excess water.

Meanwhile, slice the cucumber into very thin half-rounds (about 2 mm/⅛ in thick – use a mandoline if you have one), then rub the salt, ginger and lime zest (if using) into the cucumbers and leave to sit for 20–30 minutes to tenderise.

Rinse the cucumber mixture under cold running water and squeeze out any excess water. Toss the cucumber and wakame together in the seasoned vinegar.

You can serve this immediately but it is perhaps more delicious after a few hours in the refrigerator, so the veg absorbs the dressing. It will keep for about a week in the refrigerator, but I'd say it peaks at about 3 days.

DIFFICULTY
Very very not difficult

JACKFRUIT KARAAGE
(CRISPY FRIED JACKFRUIT)

SERVES 2

Our legendary old head chef at Nanban, Rivaaj Maharaj, grew up in an Indian household in South Africa, where jackfruit was a staple, and it was Rivaaj who came up with this recipe: jackfruit deep-fried in the style of Japanese fried chicken, which is nothing short of genius. Jackfruit is now widely used as a meat substitute in stews and curries but I prefer it in recipes like this, where it's kept more intact so you can fully appreciate its toothsome texture and subtle artichoke-like flavour. It is, in fact, so 'meaty' that every now and again a customer will send this dish back to the kitchen, mistakenly thinking we'd served them chicken!

1 × 400 g (14 oz) tin young green jackfruit, drained
cornflour (cornstarch) or seasoned flour (see below), for dredging
at least 1 litre (34 fl oz/4 cups) oil, for deep-frying
salt and freshly ground black pepper (optional)

MARINADE

4 tablespoons sake
2 tablespoons mirin
2 tablespoons soy sauce
1 tablespoon vinegar
juice of 1 lime
1 tablespoon sesame oil
1 tablespoon sriracha or similar hot chilli sauce
10 garlic cloves, peeled
2 shallots or 1 banana shallot, roughly chopped
15 g (⅔ oz) fresh root ginger (peeled weight), thinly sliced
½ teaspoon salt
¼ teaspoon black pepper
¼ teaspoon dashi powder

SEASONED FLOUR (OPTIONAL)

200 g (7 oz/2 cups) cornflour (cornstarch)
1 tablespoon sesame seeds
1 teaspoon black pepper
1 teaspoon salt
¼ teaspoon chilli powder
¼ teaspoon ground ginger

For the marinade, whizz all the ingredients together in a food processor until no big chunks remain (it doesn't have to be perfectly smooth).

If there are any really big chunks of jackfruit, cut them a bit smaller – they shouldn't be bite-size, but probably not much bigger than two-bite size. Coat the jackfruit in the marinade and leave in the refrigerator for at least 2 hours, and up to 3 days.

For the seasoned flour (if using), stir together all the ingredients until the seasonings are well distributed.

To cook, pour the oil into a very deep, wide saucepan, to come no higher than halfway up the sides and heat to 180°C (350°F). Remove the jackfruit from the marinade, letting any excess drip off, and dredge in the cornflour or seasoned flour, ensuring that all the nooks and crannies are well coated – this will help maximise crunch and help keep the sugars in the marinade from burning. Carefully lower the jackfruit into the oil in small batches, checking the temperature periodically to ensure it is still around 180°C (350°F), and fry for about 5 minutes, until the crust is golden brown.

Remove the jackfruit with a slotted spoon and drain on paper towels; if you're not using the seasoned flour, finish with a few pinches of salt and pepper. Serve with Vegan Japanese Mayo (page 43), Ponzu (page 44), or just good old soy sauce and perhaps a wedge of lemon.

DIFFICULTY

It is difficult for some people to believe this is vegan, but it's not difficult to make

SWEET CRUNCHY VEGETABLES, KINPIRA-STYLE
(KINPIRA YASAI)

SERVES 4

One of my favourite simple Japanese sides are crunchy vegetables cooked in a style called *kinpira*, in which the veg are stir-fried with soy sauce, mirin, sesame and chilli until the liquid reduces to a thick, sticky glaze. It's typically done with burdock or lotus root, which are great if you can get them, but pretty much any crunchy veg with a bit of sweetness works well. This is delicious hot and fresh from the pan, but it's also really good cold, making it ideal bento fodder (page 170).

2 tablespoons vegetable oil
1 dried red chilli, cut into slivers, or a pinch of chilli flakes
4 carrots, peeled, halved and cut at an angle into strips about 3 mm (⅛ in) thick
150–200 g (5–7 oz) tenderstem broccoli, cut in half
100–150 g (3½–5 oz) mangetout (snow peas), snap peas or fine beans
1 red (bell) pepper, sliced about 3 mm (⅛ in) thick
4 tablespoons soy sauce
2 tablespoons mirin
1 tablespoon light brown sugar
1 tablespoon white sesame seeds
2 teaspoons sesame oil

Heat the oil and the chilli in a large frying pan (skillet) or wok over a high heat. When the chilli begins to sizzle, add all the veg and stir-fry for a few minutes, until they begin to tenderise. Add the soy sauce, mirin and sugar, mix well and cook until the liquid has reduced to a thick glaze. Add the sesame seeds and sesame oil and stir through. Remove from the heat and leave to cool slightly before serving (it's better closer to room temperature), or transfer to the refrigerator and eat within 5 days.

DIFFICULTY
Stupidly not difficult

LEEK, PEA AND POTATO CROQUETTES
(YASAI KOROKKE)

MAKES 16 CROQUETTES, WHICH IS A LOT
(ENOUGH FOR 4 SERVINGS AS A MAIN, 8 AS A SIDE), BUT THEY FREEZE WELL

European croquettes are usually béchamel-based, which makes them tricky for vegans – but come to think of it, they're actually tricky for everyone because béchamel is so delicate. Japanese croquettes side-step issues of both dairy and technique through the magic of potatoes, which are easy to cook and to shape – and they're plants! Yay plants! You can put pretty much any veg you like in here (in Japan bits of carrot and cabbage are common), but for me the combination of leeks and peas is pure comfort food.

1 kg (2 lb 4 oz) floury potatoes, peeled and cut into
2.5 cm (1 in) chunks
2 tablespoons olive oil
2 leeks, diced
150 g (5 oz) peas
salt and pepper, to taste
vegan egg replacer, equivalent to 8 eggs, prepared according to the manufacturers' instructions, or 2 x recipe quantity of Batter for Breadcrumbing (page 46)
about 80 g (3 oz/scant ⅔ cup) plain (all-purpose) flour, for dredging
about 150 g (5 oz/3½ cups) panko breadcrumbs
about 2 litres (70 fl oz/8 cups) oil, for deep-frying (or less for shallow-frying)

Boil the potatoes until fork-tender, 10–15 minutes, then drain and leave to cool slightly.

Meanwhile, sauté the leeks in the oil over a medium-high heat until they soften, then add the peas and continue to cook for a few minutes until they become tender but not soft.

Mash the potatoes and fold in the leeks and peas, seasoning the mixture generously with salt and pepper. When the mash is cool enough to handle, divide it into 16 equal balls and then squash each ball into a kind of oblong patty shape. Lay the potato patties out on baking sheets lined with kitchen foil and transfer to the freezer to firm up for about 30 minutes.

Meanwhile, prepare the egg replacer or batter.

Dredge the patties in the flour, then dip in the egg replacer or batter, and then the panko, ensuring they are all well-coated. At this point the croquettes can be frozen on the baking sheets to be enjoyed later, or cooked straight away (the cooking process is the same from frozen or chilled).

Preheat your oven to 100°C (210°F/Gas ½). Heat the oil in a wide, deep saucepan to 180°C (350°F).

Carefully lower the croquettes into the hot oil, in batches of 4–6, and fry until deep golden brown, about 8 minutes. Remove with a slotted spoon, drain on a wire rack and keep hot in the oven with the oven door slightly open, until ready to serve.

ALTERNATIVE METHOD

Preheat the oven to 200°C (400°F/Gas 7).

Pour enough oil into a non-stick, flat-bottomed frying pan (skillet) to come up to a depth of 5 mm (¼ in) and place over a medium-high heat. Carefully lower in the croquettes and fry on each side for about 5 minutes, until golden brown.

Transfer the par-fried croquettes to a baking sheet and bake in the oven for 15–20 minutes, until a thin knife inserted into the middle of a croquette comes out feeling hot to the touch.

Enjoy with plenty of Tonkatsu Sauce (page 47), Ponzu (page 44) or ketchup.

DIFFICULTY
Ridiculously not difficult

SWEETCORN CURRY CROQUETTES
(KARĒ KOROKKE)

MAKES 16 CROQUETTES, WHICH IS A LOT
(ENOUGH FOR 4 SERVINGS AS A MAIN, 8 AS A SIDE), BUT THEY FREEZE WELL

In Japan, they have something called curry pan, or curry bread, which is essentially an oblong doughnut filled with Japanese curry, so you can have curry in a convenient hand-held format. That recipe is nice, but it's a bit tricky for a book called *Vegan JapanEasy* (maybe my next book will be called *Vegan Japanslightlymoredifficult*), so here's an alternative: curry croquettes, which are perhaps even better because they're more crunchy on the outside. Win-win!

1 kg (2 lb 4 oz) floury potatoes, peeled and
    cut into 2.5 cm (1 in) chunks
2 tablespoons oil
1 onion, finely diced
1 hot red chilli, finely diced
150 g (5 oz) sweetcorn (from a tin is fine)
2 heaped tablespoons curry powder
1 heaped tablespoon garam masala
salt, to taste
vegan egg replacer, equivalent to 8 eggs,
    prepared according to the manufacturers'
    instructions, or 2 x recipe quantity of Batter
    for Breadcrumbing (page 46)
about 80 g (3 oz/scant ⅔ cup) plain (all-purpose)
    flour, for dredging
about 150 g (5 oz/3½ cups) panko breadcrumbs
about 2 litres (70 fl oz/8 cups) oil, for deep-frying
    (or less for shallow-frying)

Boil the potatoes until fork-tender, 10–15 minutes, then drain and leave to cool slightly.

Meanwhile, sauté the onions and chilli in the oil over a medium-high heat until they soften, then add the corn and continue to cook for several minutes until everything starts to brown a bit. Add the spices and cook for another few minutes to make a thick paste, then remove from the heat.

Mash the potatoes and stir in the onion-corn-spice mixture, and add a generous amount of salt. When the mash is cool enough to handle, divide it into 16 equal balls and then squash each ball into a kind of oblong patty shape. Lay the potato patties out on baking sheets lined with foil and transfer to the freezer to firm up for about 30 minutes.

Meanwhile, prepare the egg replacer or batter.

Dredge the patties in the flour, then dip in the egg replacer or batter, and then the panko, ensuring they are all well-coated. At this point the croquettes can be frozen on the baking sheets, or cooked straight away. (The cooking process is the same from frozen or chilled.)

Preheat your oven to 100°C (210°F/Gas ½). Heat the oil in a wide, deep saucepan to 180°C (350°F).

Carefully lower the croquettes into the hot oil, in batches of 4–6, and fry until deep golden brown, about 8 minutes. Remove with a slotted spoon, drain on a wire rack and keep hot in the oven with the oven door slightly open, until ready to serve.

ALTERNATIVE METHOD

Preheat the oven to 200°C (400°F/Gas 7).

Pour enough oil into a non-stick, flat-bottomed frying pan (skillet) to come up to a depth of 5 mm (¼ in) and place over a medium-high heat. Carefully lower in the croquettes and fry on each side for about 5 minutes, until golden brown.

Transfer the par-fried croquettes to a baking sheet and bake in the oven for 15–20 minutes, until a thin knife inserted into the middle of a croquette comes out feeling hot to the touch.

DIFFICULTY
Super not difficult

FRIED BABY AUBERGINE SOAKED IN DASHI
(NASUBI AGEBITASHI)

MAKES 4 LITTLE SERVINGS, 2 MEDIUM-SIZED SERVINGS,
OR 1 TIM ANDERSON-SIZED SERVING

My mum hates aubergines (eggplants) – it's a 'texture thing', she says – and since she did all the cooking when I was growing up, we never ate them. So of course when I was a teenager I rebelled by going to seedy ethnic restaurants in downtown Milwaukee to gorge on forbidden moussaka, ratatouille and melanzane parmigiana. While the other kids at school were having sex and drinking, I was freebasing baba ghanoush with vegan punks in Turkish restaurant bathroom cubicles.

Not really. As far as I can recall, I had no feelings one way or another about aubergines when I was a kid, mainly because I rarely even encountered them. But over the years I've had so many fantastic, memorable aubergine dishes that it's now quite possibly my favourite vegetable: breaded and fried and draped over pizza; stir-fried 'yu xiang'-style with zingy Sichuan seasonings; braised with tomatoes, capers and olives in a rich caponata; or as *nasubi agebitashi*, this simple and classic Japanese dish of fried aubergines soaked in a seasoned dashi. I find these so irresistibly delicious that I can't help myself from snacking on them periodically as they marinate in the refrigerator, like dipping into a jar of pickles. But, of course, the longer you leave them the better they get, literally gushing with flavour. And they are exceptionally easy to make.

about 400 g (14 oz) baby aubergines (eggplants) (8–10 pieces)
oil, for shallow-frying
200–250 ml (7–8½ fl oz/scant 1–1 cup) Vegan Tsuyu (page 37)
10 g (½ oz) fresh root ginger, peeled and finely grated (shredded)
150 g (5 oz) daikon/mooli (or radishes), peeled, grated and squeezed to remove excess water
1 spring onion (scallion), finely sliced

Score the skin of each aubergine on both sides by making little shallow cuts at an angle, spaced no more than 3 mm (⅛ in) apart – this is partly decorative but it also improves the aubergines' texture and helps them absorb the dashi and cook more quickly.

Heat a generous 5 mm (¼ in) depth of oil in a large frying pan (skillet) over a medium heat, then add the aubergines in a single layer (you may have to do this in batches). Fry for 12–15 minutes, turning the aubergines often, to make sure they cook evenly, until their skins are brittle and glossy and they are soft enough to cut with a spoon. Remove from the oil and drain very well on paper towels – I always drain them on a couple of layers of paper towels, then change the towels and drain them again. Leave the aubergines to cool.

Meanwhile, bring the tsuyu and the ginger to a simmer in a small saucepan, then remove from the heat.

Pack the aubergines into a container and pour over the tsuyu – it should just barely cover them (but don't worry if it doesn't quite). Leave the aubergines to soak in the tsuyu in the refrigerator for at least 8 hours, and up to 4 days.

Serve chilled or at room temperature, garnished with the grated daikon and sliced spring onion.

DIFFICULTY
Delightfully not difficult

FRIED TOFU IN DASHI
(AGEDASHI TOFU)

SERVES 2, OR PERHAPS 4 IF PART OF A MUCH LARGER MEAL;
1 IF IT'S A 'MAIN DISH'

If you're enchanted by the 'light and delicate' side of Japanese cuisine, this recipe is for you, because it don't get much more light and delicate than this: cloud-like puffs of fried silken tofu, crisp on the outside and pillowy-soft in the middle, half-soaked in a limpid dashi sauce. I'm really more of an 'extreme spicy cheese ramen' kind of guy, but even I must say that there is something wonderfully soothing about this soft, subtle and satisfying dish.

1 block (about 350 g/12 oz) firm silken tofu
at least 1 litre (34 fl oz/4 cups) oil, for deep-frying
about 80 g (3 oz/generous ¾ cup) potato starch or
   cornflour (cornstarch), for dredging
1 cm (½ in) piece of fresh root ginger, peeled and
   finely grated (shredded)
50 g (2 oz) daikon, peeled and finely grated
   (shredded)
1 spring onion (scallion), finely sliced
a pinch each of white and black sesame seeds

DASHI SAUCE
200 ml (7 fl oz/scant 1 cup) dashi (any kind,
   pages 33–34)
1 tablespoon cornflour (cornstarch)
1 tablespoon soy sauce
1 tablespoon mirin
1 teaspoon rice vinegar

Gently press the excess water from the tofu by placing it in a container or dish with a plate on top of it, and something on top of the plate to weigh it down (a tin of tomatoes works well). Leave it for about 1 hour, then pat it dry with paper towels.

Meanwhile, make the dashi sauce. Combine 1 tablespoon of the dashi with the cornflour and stir together to make a slurry. Combine the remaining dashi, soy sauce, mirin and vinegar in a saucepan and bring to a low boil. Stir in the cornflour mixture and simmer for a minute or two to thicken, then remove from the heat and leave to cool (I think it's best at room temperature, but it's good hot or cold as well).

Pour the oil into a very deep, wide saucepan, to come no higher than halfway up the sides and heat to 180°C (350°F).

Cut the drained tofu into 6 blocks and dredge each one gently in the potato starch or cornflour. Deep-fry for 5–7 minutes until golden brown, then remove with a slotted spoon and drain on paper towels.

Mix the ginger and daikon together and squeeze to expel excess moisture.

To serve, place the tofu cubes in a shallow dish. Pour the dashi sauce around the tofu so that the bottom soaks up the sauce but the top remains crispy. Finish with the daikon-ginger mixture, sliced spring onions and a pinch or two of sesame seeds.

DIFFICULTY
Fiendishly not difficult

GYOZA

I'm sure you've seen those pop-sci articles about how to spot a psychopath, like how they don't yawn when other people yawn or how they watch *Love Island*. Well here's another dead giveaway: only psychopaths don't love gyoza. This is 100 per cent true. Or maybe not, I don't know, I'm not a psychologist. But I am an experienced gyozologist and if there's one thing my years of study has taught me, it's that gyoza is beloved by all decent human beings. What's not to love about steamy little parcels of dough, supple on top and crispy on the bottom, stuffed with juicy and flavourful fillings.

Making gyoza takes a bit of practise, but it's not hard - and once you find your groove, crimping and folding them becomes a pleasantly mindless repetitive task, like a kind of meditation. Or, if you are making a lot of gyoza, you can get your friends and family involved and it becomes a really fun, chatty, social experience (gyoza is a great conduit for gossip). Oh yes and gyoza is even easier if you buy the pre-made frozen wrappers – not a cheat, at all, as this is how most people in Japan make them, but you will have to go to an Asian supermarket to find them.

Otherwise, here is the gyoza dough recipe. I'm notoriously bad at pastry but I still find this easy, and it's made from really basic storecupboard ingredients that you probably already have.

And remember: ugly gyoza are still delicious, so don't worry if your pleats aren't perfect. It's all about that inner beauty.

GYOZA WRAPPER DOUGH

MAKES 40 GYOZA WRAPPERS

280 g (10 oz/generous 2 cups) plain
  (all-purpose) flour
½ teaspoon salt
120 ml (4 fl oz/½ cup) just-boiled water
cornflour (cornstarch), as needed for dusting

Stir the flour and salt together in a mixing bowl. Add the boiled water to the flour little by little, incorporating it with a spoon or spatula as you go. When all the water has been added, start working it with your hands; when it comes together, it should be soft and very dry; in fact, it will probably seem too dry. That's fine, because it will hydrate more as it rests. Tip the dough out onto the work surface and dust it with a little cornflour. Knead for about 10 minutes, until the dough is smooth. (If you have a stand mixer with a dough hook, by all means use it – it should only take a few minutes for it to come together.)

Roll the dough out into 2 chubby logs, about 2.5 cm (1 in) in diameter. Wrap each log in cling film (plastic wrap) and leave to rest in the refrigerator for 30–60 minutes.

Unwrap the dough – it should be nice and firm but less dry at this point. Sprinkle a little more cornflour on your work surface, then cut each log into coins about 5 mm (¼ in) thick – you should get 20 pieces out of each log. Use your hands to roll each piece of dough into a little ball, then roll each ball out on the work surface into flat discs. Try to make them very thin, but not so thin that they become difficult to work with – 1 mm thick is a good goal, but 2 mm will be fine. Dust each wrapper with cornflour and stack them up as you go, covering the stack with a clean, slightly damp dish towel to keep them from drying out. If not using immediately, you can keep them in the refrigerator, wrapped in cling film, for about 3 days.

DIFFICULTY
Fiddly little guys, gyoza, but not what I'd call difficult

KIMCHI AND TOFU GYOZA FILLING

MAKES ENOUGH TO FILL 20-24 GYOZA

Tofu and kimchi are like the good cop/bad cop of food. One is meek and timid, the other aggro and unhinged. Together they balance each other perfectly (see also: Kimchi Miso Hotpot, page 123) for a superb gyoza filling.

200 g (7 oz) firm (cotton) tofu, cut into small dice
120 g (4 oz) kimchi, finely chopped
2 garlic cloves, minced (ground)
10 g (½ oz) fresh root ginger, peeled and
    minced (ground)
1 tablespoon oil
1 tablespoon sesame oil
1 tablespoon white sesame seeds
2 spring onions (scallions), finely sliced
1 tablespoon plain (all-purpose) flour
salt and chilli powder, to taste

Combine everything except the spring onions, flour, salt and chilli powder in a bowl and mix well. Transfer to a frying pan (skillet) and stir-fry over a medium-high heat for about 10 minutes – this is mainly to dry out the ingredients but also to soften the garlic and ginger. When the mixture is quite dry and starting to colour, remove from the heat and stir in the spring onions and flour.

Tip out into a bowl and leave to cool until you can handle it, then use your hands to mix it up and break the tofu into little crumbs (some big chunks are okay, but too many and the filling won't stick together). Taste and adjust the flavour with salt and chilli powder, if you like. Assemble and cook the gyoza as per the instructions overleaf.

GARLICKY MUSHROOM AND BAMBOO SHOOT GYOZA FILLING

MAKES ENOUGH TO FILL 20-24 GYOZA

I don't like it when vegan recipes attempt to mimic meat – vegetables are delicious enough in and of themselves, thank you – but when I tried this recipe I couldn't help but think, damn, that is MEATY. It's not that you could trick people into thinking these were made of pork, it's just that they have a similar juiciness and a flavour that's just as deep and satisfying.

250 g (9 oz) mushrooms (just about any kind will do,
    but I think oyster are nice), finely chopped
120 g (4 oz) bamboo shoots, finely chopped
    (use a Japanese brand if you can)
1 tablespoon sesame oil
1 tablespoon nutritional yeast
pinch of white pepper
15 g (⅔ oz) fresh root ginger, peeled and minced
    (ground)
2 tablespoons oil
8 garlic cloves, minced (ground) or finely chopped
1 tablespoon plain (all-purpose) flour
½ teaspoon brown sugar
salt, to taste

Combine the mushrooms, bamboo shoots, sesame oil, yeast flakes, white pepper and ginger in a bowl and mix well. Heat the vegetable oil in a frying pan (skillet) over a medium heat, add the garlic and sauté until barely golden brown, then add the mushroom mixture and continue to cook, stirring often, until the mushrooms have lost most of their moisture and have cooked down to about a third of their original size. Stir in the flour and brown sugar. Taste, and add salt as needed. Assemble and cook the gyoza as per the instructions overleaf.

ASSEMBLING AND COOKING GYOZA

To make gyoza, you'll need 6 things at hand: the filling, the wrappers, a small bowl of water, a baking sheet lined with baking parchment or dusted with cornflour (cornstarch), a small spoon and a slightly damp dish towel or paper towel.

Lay out a few gyoza wrappers on your counter (I don't know why, but I always do either 4 or 6 at a time). Wet your fingertips with the water, then dampen the edge of each wrapper (don't use too much water or they will become unworkably soft). Spoon a little filling into the middle of each wrapper (a generous tablespoonful is all you need), then fold the wrapper over the filling and seal. There are 2 ways I advise doing this:

1
THE NOT TRADITIONAL BUT TOTALLY EASY WAY THAT STILL MAKES VERY CUTE GYOZA

Fold the wrappers over the filling and pinch them shut to make little half-moon shapes – no need to crimp or pleat them, but make sure the seal is very tight. Then, simply curl the ends of the half-moons around to meet each other and pinch them together, so you end up with shapes like tortelloni.

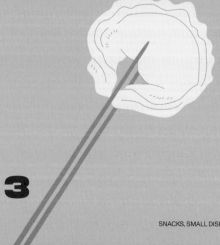

1

2

3

THE TRADITIONAL AND SOMEWHAT MORE DIFFICULT WAY THAT WILL IMPRESS YOUR JAPANESE MOTHER-IN-LAW

Fold the wrappers over the filling, but don't seal them. Instead, pinch the wrapper shut at one end. Then, use the index finger of your dominant hand to keep the filling 'tucked in' as you crimp and pinch the wrapper to seal; use your thumb to pleat the side of the wrapper closest to you, and with each pleat, pinch it firmly onto the opposite side of the wrapper. You should get about five pleats into each gyoza before you reach the other end, then simply pinch that corner shut to finish it off. This will result in lovely, traditionally crescent-shaped gyoza.

Line the gyoza up on your papered or floured baking sheet, seal-side up, so they have nice flat bottoms, and keep them covered with a damp cloth as you work so they don't dry out. When all the gyoza are done you can wrap them in cling film (plastic wrap) and keep them in the refrigerator until ready to cook, but I wouldn't recommend keeping them for much more than a day, because they tend to go soggy. (You can also freeze them at this point, on the tray, ensuring none of them are sticking together when you do. Once frozen solid, transfer them to a container or plastic bag and cook them from frozen using the same instructions as below.)

COOKING

To cook the gyoza, you will need 3 things: about 1 tablespoon of oil, a reliably non-stick pan with a snug-fitting lid, and about 100 ml (3½ fl oz/scant ½ cup) water.

Heat the oil in the pan over a high heat and add the gyoza (cook as many as you can fit, or as few as you need – the rest can be frozen). When the gyoza are sizzling, pour in the water and place the lid on the pan. Steam for 5 minutes with the lid on, then remove the lid and let all the water evaporate away. The gyoza should have nice crispy golden-brown bottoms – you can lift one up to check, and if they're still quite pale when the water is gone, just keep cooking them for another couple of minutes. Tip the gyoza out onto a plate, and serve with Ponzu (page 44) or 'gyoza sauce': 3 parts soy sauce to 1 part vinegar with a little drizzle of chilli oil or sesame oil.

VEGAN SUSHI

DIFFICULTY Not difficult, unless you try to open a vegan sushi
restaurant in Japan, in which case, good luck to you

'Vegan sushi' is one of those phrases that really rankles my cankles; I have
an automatic, irrationally negative reaction to it, and whenever anybody
says it, it makes me want to knee them in the groin and run away. This is
because in my mind sushi just isn't vegan – it's all about the fish. Right?

Actually no. I mean yes, traditionally, of course it is. The idea of 'vegan sushi'
would probably annoy most sushi chefs, or at the very least make them
chuckle bemusedly. But really, sushi is in many ways just as much about
the rice and seasonings as it is about the fish. Besides, having tried and
tested many variations of vegan sushi for this book, I am now convinced it
can be genuinely delicious, providing the same range of colours, textures
and flavours that you'd expect from a traditionally fishy sushi dinner. I may
be a purist when it comes to sushi, but even I must say that the following
recipes are some truly tasty morsels – and they look great, too.

SUSHI RICE

MAKES ABOUT 600 G (1 LB 5 OZ/3 CUPS) COOKED SUSHI RICE,
ENOUGH FOR ROUGHLY 30 PIECES OF SUSHI

Sushi rice is perhaps the most important part of any sushi, vegan or otherwise. Getting it just right may take some practice, but just keep these principles in mind and you should be able to make rice that's really quite good, and definitely better than almost any pre-packaged sushi you'd find at supermarkets or high-street chains.

TEXTURE

Sushi rice should be firm, but of course not chalky, and never mushy. Following the instructions below should get you the right doneness, but remember that how you handle the rice will also affect its texture. When you're tossing sushi rice with its seasoning, use a cutting-and-folding motion rather than a digging motion; and when you're shaping sushi, don't squeeze it with a death grip – use just enough pressure to get it to stick together.

TEMPERATURE

One of the worst things about shop-bought sushi is that the rice is too damn cold. This makes it go hard (unless the rice is initially overcooked) and also deadens its flavour. Sushi rice should be body temperature, or ever so slightly warm – think of sushi as a bit like an open-faced sandwich: non-carby thing on carby thing. And you'd never make a sandwich with refrigerator-cold bread, that's just weird and gross.

SEASONING

Sushi rice needs to be seasoned with sushi vinegar, and plenty of it, while it's still hot so the grains can absorb it properly. Yes, you'll have flavourful toppings and soy sauce on the side, but the rice should be deliciously tangy and salty on its own.

'PERFECT IS THE ENEMY OF GOOD.'

VOLTAIRE

You may not make perfect sushi rice on your first try (or maybe ever, let's be real), but the good news is it doesn't have to be perfect – it just has to be good.

And here's how to make it good.

300 g (10½ oz/1½ cups) rice, washed
390 ml (13¾ fl oz/1⅔ cups) water
5 tablespoons Seasoned Vinegar (page 41)
big pinch of sea salt

Cook the rice according to the instructions on page 26, but give it a little extra washing – you want nice, distinct grains here, so rinse away as much excess starch as you have the patience for.

Once the rice is cooked, spread it out in a large, shallow bowl or roasting pan and sprinkle over the seasoned vinegar and sea salt. Mix the vinegar through the rice using a rice paddle or spatula with slicing and turning motions. Allow the rice to cool slightly, then return to the pan it was cooked in and place the lid back on to keep it warm until you're ready to use it.

NIGIRIZUSHI

Nigirizushi are the sushi that are just a little pillow of rice with something on top, as opposed to *makizushi,* which are the rolls. They are arguably harder to make, requiring a little practise to get the technique down, but if I can make them, then so can you. Yes, I cook Japanese food for a living, but mainly noodles – I'm not a trained sushi chef and if I tried to work in a proper *sushi-ya* I would be kicked out, angrily, after about 5 minutes. My *nigiri* skills are frankly appalling. But do I let that stop me? I do not.

To make nigiri, have your cooked, body-temperature rice and a little bowl of salted water handy. Wet your hands with the water, then grab a little ball of rice – about the size of a ping-pong ball, and give it a little squeeze, using a cupping motion with your palm, to compress it into an oblong about 4 cm (1½ in) long and 1.5–2 cm (¾ in) wide.

Place a slice of the topping you're using in the palm of your non-dominant hand, and place the oblong of rice on top of it (basically, you're making the sushi upside down). Use the index and middle fingers of your dominant hand to press down along the entire length of the sushi while clenching the palm of your other hand to firmly squash everything together ('nigiri', by the way, means 'pressed') – the topping should be firmly in place, and the bottom surface of the rice should be nice and flat, so the sushi doesn't fall over when you put it on a plate.

Each of the following recipes makes 8 pieces of sushi, which will use about a quarter of the sushi rice recipe (page 108). So you can either try all 4 from a single batch of rice, or mix and match them however you like.

NIGIRIZUSHI

ROASTED RED PEPPER NIGIRI

This is one of my favourite vegan sushi, not just because of its lovely sweet flavour, but because the peeled peppers look a hell of a lot like fresh *maguro*, supple and strikingly red.

1 large red (bell) pepper
2 tablespoons soy sauce
1 tablespoon mirin
juice of ¼ lemon
¼ x recipe quantity prepared Sushi Rice (page 108)
about 1 cm (½ in) piece of fresh root ginger, peeled and grated (shredded)
a few chives, finely chopped

Place the pepper on a baking sheet under a hot grill (broiler). Cook for 10–12 minutes, turning frequently, until all of its skin is blistered and browned, and blackened in places. Remove the pepper and transfer to a plastic bag, then leave to sit in its own steam for about 10 minutes. Peel off the skin of the pepper, and tear out the stem and seeds, making sure to remove any stray seeds hiding inside. Cut the pepper into 8 neat rectangles – the best way to do this is to cut off the bottom, then cut down one side of the pepper and 'unroll' it into a long sheet. Toss the pepper slices in the soy sauce, mirin and lemon juice and leave to marinate for a while, ideally at least 1 hour. Make into nigiri as per the instructions on page 109, and garnish each piece with a little bit of ginger and chives.

TURMERIC TOFU 'TAMAGOYAKI'

I devised this to mimic *tamagoyaki*, the perennial favourite omelette sushi. It doesn't really taste like egg, but it does look like it, and it has a similar texture. Hey, two out of three ain't bad!

1 tablespoon mirin
1 teaspoon ground turmeric
big pinch of salt
180 g (6½ oz) cotton (firm) tofu, cut into 8 rectangles about 2 cm (¾ in) wide, 5 mm (¼ in) deep and 5 cm (2 in) long
1 teaspoon oil
¼ x recipe quantity prepared Sushi Rice (page 108)
½ sheet of nori, cut into strips about 1 cm (½ in) wide and 10–12 cm (4–4½ in) long

Stir together the mirin, turmeric and salt, pour over the tofu and gently toss to make sure it is evenly coated. Leave to marinate for at least 30 minutes. Heat the oil in a non-stick pan over a high heat, and cook the tofu for a couple minutes on each side, until slightly browned. Remove from the heat, leave to cool and make into nigiri as per the instructions on page 109. Wrap a strip of nori around each piece of sushi, using a little bit of water to secure the ends in place on the bottom of the rice.

PONZU-GRILLED MUSHROOM NIGIRI

Good-quality mushrooms in Japan are often served simply grilled (barbecued) with just a little fresh lime and sea salt to season. The combination of citrus and mushroom may sound a bit odd, but it really works – the acidity of lime is the perfect accent to the deep, earthy umami of fungi.

4 large chestnut (cremini) mushrooms or similar, destemmed and halved
1 tablespoon soy sauce
1 teaspoon sesame oil
finely grated zest and juice of ½ lime
¼ x recipe quantity prepared Sushi Rice (page 108)

Toss the mushrooms in the soy sauce, sesame oil and lime juice. Grill (broil) on high, gill-side up, until slightly shrivelled and browned on top. Make into nigiri as per the instructions on page 109, and garnish with the lime zest.

'UNAGI'-STYLE FRIED AUBERGINE NIGIRI

For most of my life, unagi (freshwater eel) was my favourite sushi. Then I learned that unagi is basically endangered due to overfishing and climate change. So, no more eel for me. Luckily, this squidgy fried aubergine version – which has a similar soft, fatty texture to eel – is just as delicious, and about a million times more sustainable.

½ aubergine (eggplant), or 2–4 baby aubergines
oil, for shallow-frying
¼ x recipe quantity prepared Sushi Rice (page 108)
wasabi, as needed
3–4 tablespoons Sweet Soy Sauce (page 40)
white sesame seeds, to garnish
sansho pepper, to garnish (optional)

If it's a big aubergine, cut it into 8 batons or wedges about 6 cm (2½ in) long and 2 cm (¾ in) across. For baby aubergines, just cut them in half, or quarters if they are large. Score the aubergines' skin with short slashes every 2 mm (¹⁄₁₆ in) or so.

Fry the aubergine in a 1 cm (½ in) depth of oil over a medium-high heat, until completely soft. Drain and blot dry with paper towels.

Apply a dab of wasabi to each pillow of rice before proceeding to top with the fried aubergine, then make into nigiri, as per the instructions on page 109. Brush over the sweet soy sauce.

Ideally, bust out the blowtorch and flame each nigiri until the sauce bubbles and caramelises – but if you don't have a blowtorch, no worries, this will still be good without it. Garnish each piece with the sesame and sansho.

MAKIZUSHI

Let's rock some rolls. *Makizushi,* or sushi rolls, are where you're most likely to find vegan options within the realm of traditional sushi, often utilising pickles or otherwise crunchy veg, for a nice textural contrast to the rice. But I reckon we can do a bit better than just cucumber or dried gourd, don't you? These recipes are actually some of the most delicious sushi I've ever made – you won't miss the fish.

For each sushi roll (which makes 6 pieces), you'll need 100 g (3½ oz/ ½ cup) cooked rice (from 50 g/2 oz/¼ cup uncooked), half a sheet of nori and a bowl of water. You'll also need a piece of paper, wrapped up in a few layers of cling film (plastic wrap). Yes, really. (You can use a sushi mat if you have one, but if you don't, don't bother, unless you plan on making sushi with some regularity.) The technique is the same, but the order is slightly different for each roll, so the instructions follow below.

These recipes each make 3 rolls, or 18 pieces, out of 300 g (10½ oz/1½ cups) cooked rice – so a half batch of the sushi recipe provided on page 108.

MAKIZUSHI

SWEET POTATO PONZU ROLL

1 big sweet potato, washed
3 tablespoons Ponzu (page 44)
1½ sheets of nori
½ x recipe quantity prepared Sushi Rice (page 108)
a few chives
a few pinches of black and/or white sesame seeds

Preheat the oven to 200°C (400°F/Gas 7).

Roast the potato in its skin for 30–40 minutes, until soft throughout, then remove from the oven and let cool. When cool, peel and cut into batons about 1 cm (½ in) wide. Gently toss the potato batons in the ponzu.

Lay a half sheet of nori shiny-side down on the cling film-wrapped paper. Rub your hands with water and shake off any excess, then use your fingers to spread a third of the rice out in an even layer over the nori, leaving a gap of about 1 cm (½ in) uncovered along the far edge of the nori (you will use this to 'seal' the roll). Lay a third of the potato batons along the near side of the nori, about 1 cm (½ in) from the edge, and top with a few chives and sesame seeds.

Now we roll. Use the paper to curl up the edge of the nori, over the filling, tucking in the potatoes with your fingertips and tightening the roll as you go with gentle pressure. When you've rolled to the far edge of the nori, use a little water to dampen the exposed nori, then press the roll together to seal. With a little luck, you'll have a tight, structurally sound roll. Transfer to a cutting board and slice into 6 pieces with a sharp, wet knife.

Repeat the process to make 2 further rolls.

SPICY AVOCADO CRUNCH ROLL

1½ sheets of nori
½ x recipe quantity prepared Sushi Rice (page 108)
flesh of 1 avocado, cut into 1 cm (½ in) batons
¼ cucumber, cut into long strips no wider than
    3 mm (⅛ in)
about 100 g (3½ oz/4 cups) cornflakes, crushed
a few pinches of shichimi

Lay a half sheet of nori on your cling film-wrapped paper. Rub your hands with water and shake off any excess, then use your fingers to spread a third of the rice out in an even layer over the nori, ensuring that the rice goes right up to the edge. Now, flip the nori and the rice over so the rice is now on the bottom. Spread a little sriracha in a line along the near side of the nori, about 1 cm (½ in) from the edge, and top with a line of avocado and cucumber.

Use the paper to curl up the edge of the nori, over the filling, tucking in the avocado and cucumber with your fingertips and tightening the roll as you go with gentle pressure. When you've rolled to the far edge of the nori, press the roll together to seal. Roll the roll through the crushed cornflakes and shichimi. Transfer to a cutting board and slice into 6 pieces with a sharp, wet knife.

Repeat the process to make 2 further rolls. Be sure to roll the roll through the cornflakes just before slicing and serving – if it sits, the cornflakes will absorb moisture from the rice and go soft. So, if you're making a sushi platter, make these last!

BIG DISHES

メインディッシュ

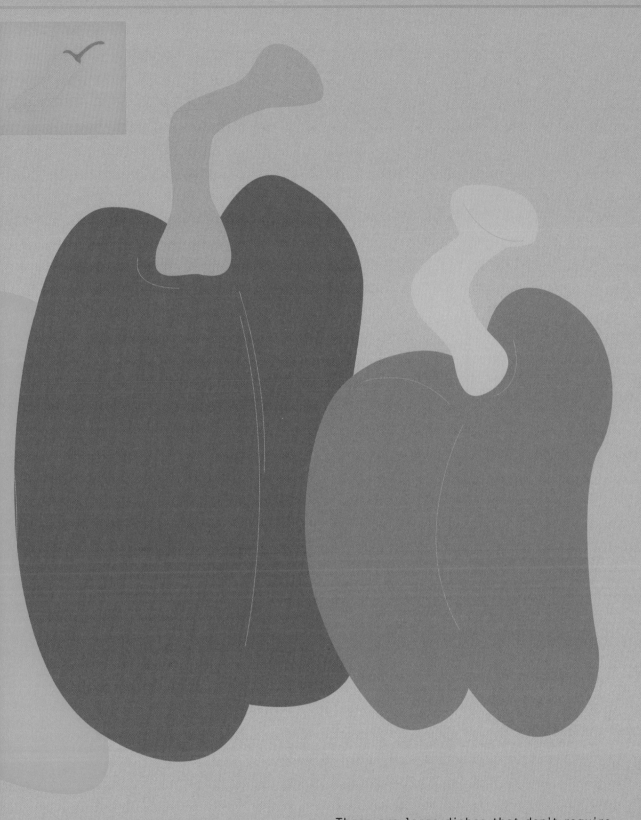

These are large dishes that don't require
anything else other than rice alongside
them to make a complete meal. Almost all
of them are one-pot recipes as well, so
even the washing-up is easy.

VEGETABLE TEMPURA

SERVES 4

Tempura is one of the greatest ways to cook vegetables in the world, and that goes for pretty much any vegetable. I mean, deep-frying in batter is always a good idea, but I think it's especially nice with fresh veg – the veg itself is essentially steamed, softening but retaining its flavour, with the light crunch of the batter adding the perfect textural complement. You can tempura-fry just about anything, so instead of putting specific vegetables in the recipe, I've just provided a few different types of vegetables and how to best prepare them for the tempura treatment.

200 g (7 oz/1½ cups) plain (all-purpose) flour, plus extra as needed
100 g (3½ oz/1 cup) cornflour (cornstarch)
pinch of salt
400 ml (13 fl oz/generous 1½ cups) sparkling water
oil, for deep-frying (about 1.5 litres/50 fl oz/6¼ cups, but possibly a little more if you're using a very wide pan). Pour your oil into a big, deep pan – it should be very wide, to accommodate a lot of ingredients, but also deep so the oil doesn't overflow. The oil should be at least 7.5 cm (3 in) deep, but it should also come up to no higher than 7.5 cm (3 in) below the rim of the pan, to be safe. Set over a medium heat while you make the batter.
various vegetables (see opposite)
100–150 ml Tsuyu (page 37), Ponzu (page 44) or Vegan Japanese Mayo (page 43), to serve

Mix together the flours and salt in a bowl, then pour in the sparkling water. Mix until the batter comes together with a consistency of double (heavy) cream. It should be badly mixed; a slightly lumpy, bubbly batter contains more air and irregularities that will give your tempura a light, lacy structure, and it also develops less gluten, which will help prevent your tempura from turning doughy and soft. I usually use chopsticks rather than a whisk to mix tempura batter to make sure it's not too well combined.

Heat the oil to 170–180°C (340–350°F). If you don't have a thermometer, simply drip a few drops of the batter into the oil to test it: if the batter sinks, it's too cold; if the batter immediately floats and sizzles, it's too hot. What you want is for the batter to sink just below the surface of the oil, then rise up and start to sizzle.

Dredge your veg in the flour and then in the batter, allowing excess to drip off before carefully placing them in the oil. KEY POINT: Many vegetables have little nooks and crannies where the batter gets trapped, like between the branches of broccoli, the hollows of cavolo nero, or the cups of mushrooms. Make sure you let as much batter drip out of these crevices as possible or the tempura will be cakey.

Use tongs or chopsticks to separate the veg as they fry so they don't stick together. You'll have to fry the veg in batches – the ideal way to serve and eat this is straight out of the fryer, so if you've got somewhere for people to sit in the kitchen, gather them around and play tempura chef for the night, serving the veg as they're ready. If that's not possible, just keep the tempura in a low oven with the door slightly ajar to let out moisture until it's all ready to serve.

The tempura is done when it is a light golden brown and hard to the touch – use tongs or chopsticks to feel if the batter has firmed up into a nice, crunchy shell before removing from the oil and draining on paper towels.

Serve with tsuyu, ponzu or Japanese mayo to dip on the side.

DIFFICULTY

¡No es difficulto!

Mushrooms: Medium-sized mushrooms, such as shiitake, chestnut (cremini) or oyster, can be cooked with basically no preparation. You will probably have to destem shiitake as they tend to be tough, but otherwise they're good to go. Enoki or shimeji are also lovely – they should be broken up into small clusters, still attached at the bottom. If you are using eringi, they should be cut into very thin slices, as they can often be tough even when fully cooked.

Broccoli and friends: If you're using normal broccoli, break it into florets that are a little bigger than bite-size; if they're too big, they may still be raw and tough in the middle. Or, you can just use tenderstem or purple sprouting broccoli, which are the perfect size and shape as they are. Cauliflower works well, too, and I especially like romanesco.

Carrots, sweet potatoes and squash: This gang need to be sliced thinly to ensure they soften by the time the batter is crisp – about 1 cm (½ in) maximum. Some varieties of squash with tender skins, such as kabocha or butternut, don't need to be peeled, as the high heat of frying will soften the skin nicely.

Aubergines (eggplant): Baby aubergines work best – slice them in half, then make a series of cuts through them on one side, so that you can splay them out into something resembling a badminton shuttlecock. If you're using a big aubergine, just cut into 1 cm (½ in) slices or wedges.

Asparagus: Asparagus is simply fantastic in tempura; just make sure you discard any woody bits, but also try not to use asparagus that's really thin – it'll become very, very soft.

Sweetcorn: There are three basic ways to do corn as tempura: you can cut it into little wheels, about 2.5 cm (1 in) wide; you can cut the ears into eighths, so you have sort-of triangular batons; or you can take the kernels off the cob (or use tinned corn, which is delicious) and do them kakiage-style. Kakiage are essentially fritters; to make them, drop the corn kernels into the batter and scoop them out with a slotted spoon. Let most of the batter drip away before pushing them off the spoon with another spoon, directly into the oil. They'll form little rafts of exquisitely crunchy, sweetcorn goodness.

Cavolo nero: Stripped away from their tough stalks, the leaves of cavolo nero make amazing tempura that are almost 100 per cent crunch. You can use kale as well, but it's hard to drain off excess batter from their leaves, so they often come out cakey.

Onions and leeks: These are essentially glorified onion rings, except they're not rings – onion discs, I guess. Cut onions no more than 7 mm (¼ in) thick, and do the same with leeks, at an angle, so they are sort of parallelogrammatic.

(Bell) Peppers: The best peppers for tempura are Padróns, or the similar (but very hard to find) Japanese shishito – just drop them in the batter and fry, no need to prep. But ordinary sweet peppers work well, too, cut into chunks or rings.

Okra: Okra done as tempura is as addictive as chips. Cut them in half lengthways to maximise crunch.

Fennel: This may seem like an odd choice for tempura, given that fennel's aniseedy flavour isn't usually found in Japanese cuisine, but most of that aroma steams away during frying, so you're left with a sweet, toothsome vegetable with only a subtle scent. Slice them thinly (about 5 mm/¼ in maximum) before frying.

There are also, I must warn you, a few vegetables I cannot recommend for tempura:

Spring onions (scallions): These always seem like such a good idea, but really they don't soften enough during frying to bite through – I always end up pulling the entire onion out of the batter, leaving behind a hollow tempura sheath.

Courgettes (zucchini): Unless you cut them very thinly and fry them for a very long time, they just have too much water in them – water that continues to seep out after frying, ultimately making the batter go soggy from within.

Tomatoes: Maybe this one's obvious, but unless the tomatoes are really firm, they fall apart in the fryer.

KIMCHI MISO HOTPOT
(KIMCHI NABE)

SERVES 4

Korean food has had a big influence on Japanese cuisine, to the extent that some Korean ingredients are now found at pretty much any Japanese supermarket. One of these ingredients is, of course, kimchi, the spicy fermented cabbage often called the national dish of Korea. In Japan, one of its most common uses is in *kimchi nabe*, a hotpot that harnesses kimchi's funky-sour-spicy-salty-umami flavour to season ingredients cooked in a light-yet-punchy broth. This is especially nice in winter.

1 tablespoon oil
1 tablespoon sesame oil
1 onion, finely sliced
80 g (3 oz) miso
2 tablespoons sake
800 ml (27 fl oz/scant 3½ cups) dashi (any kind, pages 33–34) or water
350–400 g (12–14 oz) kimchi (include a little kimchi juice in this weight)
20 g (¾ oz) fresh root ginger, peeled and finely grated (shredded)
2 tablespoons mirin
hot chilli sauce and soy sauce, to taste (or use gochu-jang, Korean fermented chilli paste, if you can get it)
400–600 g (14 oz–1 lb 5 oz) tofu, cut into blocks about 2.5 cm (1 in) thick (firm/cotton or silken tofu are both okay but I like the hearty substance of firm/cotton in this dish)
2 leeks, cut at an angle about 1 cm (½ in) thick
½ Chinese or Savoy cabbage, cored and cut into chunks about 4 cm (1¾ in) wide
400 g (14 oz) mushrooms (a mixture of shiitake, enoki and oyster are nice)
4 portions of uncooked ramen noodles or cooked rice

Heat the oils in a deep casserole (Dutch oven) or saucepan over a medium heat and sauté the onion until slightly softened. Whisk in the miso, then add the sake. Add the dashi, kimchi, ginger and mirin, and bring to the boil. Simmer for 10–15 minutes for the flavours to infuse, then taste and adjust the seasoning with chilli sauce and soy sauce as needed. (The broth will season everything else in the soup, so it should be *quite* spicy and salty.)

Arrange the tofu, leeks, cabbage and mushrooms in the soup and bring back to the boil. Boil for about 5 minutes, until the vegetables are tender. If you are using ramen noodles, put them into the broth and cook until al dente; if you are using rice, dish it out into individual bowls. Serve the hotpot in the pan at the table, so that people can serve themselves as they like.

DIFFICULTY
As not difficult as pie (kimchi pie?)

SICHUAN-STYLE HOT AND NUMBING TOFU WITH ANCIENT GRAINS

(MAPO TOFU)

SERVES 4

I am obsessed with mapo tofu. So, a couple of years ago I was so hell bent on making the perfect version that I cooked it four times *per week*. I tried many variations, including several vegan versions, but kept coming back to the classic version, with pork. This annoyed me, because the dish is so very nearly vegan, I felt like the pork was unneccessary.

Then, I realised it wasn't really the *flavour* of the pork I was missing – it was the texture that provides a nice textural contrast to the soft tofu. I had been replacing them with things like mushroom, which had a nice flavour, but they were too soft. So I tried a version with chewy wholegrains – namely freekeh – and voila! We had vegan mapo tofu lift-off!

You may be asking what this classic Sichuan recipe is doing in a Japanese book. Well, there exists in Japan a sort of domesticated version of mapo tofu, which is much less spicy and more sweet. But if I'm honest, this is the OTT hot-and-numbingness of the Sichuan original, which I love.

This recipe calls for two Chinese products for which you may need to venture to the Asian supermarket: preserved black beans and *doubanjiang* (fermented chilli bean paste). Preserved black beans have a rich, almost chocolatey, sweet-and-salty flavour, but they can be omitted if you can't get them, and doubanjiang can be replaced with miso – but you'll have to add a bit more chilli to give it the requisite kick.

The cooking time varies depending on the grain that is used. It can take as little as 10 minutes for buckwheat but up to 45 minutes for spelt.

2 packs of firm or extra firm silken tofu (600–700 g/ 1 lb 5–9 oz), cut into 2.5 cm (1 in) cubes
100 g (3½ oz/generous ½ cup) plump wholegrains (such as freekeh, buckwheat, spelt)
1½ tablespoons Sichuan peppercorns
4 dried red chillies, or 1 heaped teaspoon chilli flakes
4 tablespoons vegetable oil
1 bird's eye or similar hot chilli (or more, to taste), finely sliced

4 garlic cloves, finely sliced
10 g (½ oz) fresh root ginger (peeled weight), finely grated (shredded)
1 leek, halved and cut into 5 mm (¼ in) slices
1 tablespoon preserved black beans (optional)
80 g (3 oz) doubanjiang (Sichuan chilli bean paste)
1½ tablespoons caster (superfine) sugar
500 ml (17 fl oz/2 cups) dashi (any kind, pages 33–34)
1 tablespoon sesame oil
1½ tablespoons cornflour (cornstarch), mixed with a little water
mushroom ketchup and/or soy sauce, to taste
small handful of coriander (cilantro), roughly torn
toasted sesame seeds, for sprinkling
plenty (a lot) of sansho pepper (optional)

Bring a pan of salted water to a simmer, then add the tofu and poach for 10 minutes. Remove with a slotted spoon and transfer to a tray to air-dry.

Return the water to the boil and add the grains. Cook until al dente. Drain well and set aside.

Toast the Sichuan pepper and dried chillies in a dry frying pan (skillet) over a medium-low heat until aromatic, then remove. Leave to cool then grind to a coarse powder in a spice grinder or mortar.

Add the oil to the frying pan and place over a high heat, then add the bird's eye chilli, garlic, ginger, leek, black beans and cooked grains. Fry until the leeks soften slightly, then add the doubanjiang or miso, sugar, the ground Sichuan pepper and chilli mixture. Cook for a few minutes, stirring often. Add the dashi and sesame oil. Bring to the boil, then stir in some of the cornflour-water mixture. Let the sauce boil for a few minutes to thicken; add more cornflour if you want it thicker. Taste the sauce and adjust the seasoning with mushroom ketchup and/or soy sauce. Gently stir in the tofu to coat the tofu without breaking it up.

Serve with the coriander and sesame seeds sprinkled on top, and lots of sansho pepper.

DIFFICULTY

Fabulously not difficult

MOCK MEAT MENCHI KATSU
(BREADED AND FRIED VEGAN BURGER PATTIES)

SERVES 4

I've never been a fan of vegetarian burgers. The ones that attempt to mimic meat have never convinced me, and the ones that don't aren't burgers, they're just weird vegetable sandwiches. And what's the point, anyway? Vegetables are delicious in their own right; why try to manipulate them into something they're not? That's what I thought, anyway. But a while back I had this burger from a place called Halo Burger in Brixton, which used a new product called Beyond Meat.

It was a revelation.

It ticked all the burger boxes, a damn near perfect impression of Five Guys. The 'meat' was delicious, probably only identifiable as meat fakery if you already knew that ahead of time, and the cheese was incredible as well. I didn't know that the burger was fully vegan, not just vegetarian, before I ate it, and I couldn't believe actual cheese wasn't involved.

Of course, the lettuce, tomatoes, burger sauce and pickles may have helped obscure any tellingly 'fake' flavours and textures, but that doesn't matter – a burger is a sandwich, after all, and it's not about any one ingredient. It's about how they all come together. And this came together beautifully. It made me finally understand veggie burgers; they're meant to deliver pure, simple, nostalgic joy. The problem is, they never have before – not to me, at least. They've only delivered disappointment and sadness. But I'm not exaggerating when I say this burger was life-changing – it's like I'm through the looking glass now. If a vegan burger can be this good, anything is possible. Like a proper vegan *menchi katsu*.

Menchi katsu are kind of the poor man's tonkatsu: breaded and fried meat, but instead of a prime cut like a pork chop, they use minced (ground) meat. I figured they'd be the perfect way for me to start experimenting with mock meat in my own cooking, and I was right – they're every bit as crunchy-juicy-comforting as the traditional version.

4 vegan burger patties – I highly, *highly* recommend Beyond Meat, but if you have a brand you know you like (and that actually tastes at least vaguely of meat and not of beans), then by all means use that
60 g (2 oz/scant ½ cup) plain (all-purpose) flour
vegan egg replacer, equivalent to 4 eggs, prepared according to the manufacturers' instructions, or 1 x recipe quantity Batter for Breadcrumbing (page 46)
100–120 g (3½–4 oz/2⅓–2½ cups) panko breadcrumbs
oil, for shallow-frying
salt and black pepper, to taste

TO SERVE
½ hispi (pointed) cabbage, very finely sliced (shredded)
cooked rice or 8 slices white bread
Tonkatsu Sauce (page 47), ketchup or Vegan Japanese Mayo (page 43)

Season each patty well with salt and pepper, then dredge in the flour, then the egg replacer or batter, then the panko, then back in the egg replacer, and finally in the panko again (this will give it a super-thick, super-crunchy crust).

Heat a 1 cm (½ in) depth of oil over medium-high heat and fry the patties for about 4 minutes on each side until golden brown and crunchy (NOTE: this is assuming your burgers are cooking from chilled; if they're frozen, finish them in a 180°C (350°F/Gas 6) oven for about 10 minutes to make sure they're hot throughout).

Drain on paper towels and season again with salt and pepper. Serve with the grated cabbage, rice, and gallons and gallons of tonkatsu sauce or ketchup OR put them between two slices of white bread with the cabbage, tonkatsu sauce and some Japanese mayo for a vegan take on the ever-popular katsu sandwich.

DIFFICULTY
I can't believe it's not difficult... or not meat

VARIOUS VEGETABLES BRAISED IN DASHI
(ODEN / NIMONO)

SERVES 4

There are many variations on this type of preparation in Japanese cuisine, which fall under the umbrella term *nimono*, or 'simmered things'. Probably the most common is oden, which is sold at specialist shops or at convenience stores, with various ingredients hot-held in a light dashi to be chosen and paid for individually, topped up with the broth in a big bowl or bucket. It is extremely comforting – there's nothing like sticking your face into a billowing cloud of hot dashi vapour when it's miserably cold outside. The fact that the vegetables are always juicy and soft is almost a bonus.

1 block (400 g/14 oz) firm (cotton) tofu
oil, for shallow-frying
1.2 litres (40 fl oz/4¾ cups) dashi (any kind, pages 33–34)
4 tablespoons soy sauce
4 tablespoons mirin
4 tablespoons sake
¼ teaspoon salt
1 large carrot, peeled and cut into 4 big chunks
300 g (10½ oz) turnips, peeled and halved
1 hispi (pointed) cabbage, quartered
8 shiitake (fresh or rehydrated), destemmed, or chestnut (cremini) mushrooms
50 g (2 oz) mangetout (snow peas)
hot mustard, to serve (optional)

Cut the tofu into 4 big chunks, then slice each chunk to make 8 triangles.

Heat a 3 mm (⅛ in) depth of oil in a non-stick pan over a medium-high heat, and fry the tofu on all sides for about 10 minutes in total, until golden brown all over. Remove and drain on paper towels.

Combine the dashi, soy sauce, mirin, sake and salt in a large saucepan and bring to the boil, then add the carrots and turnips and reduce to a simmer. Cook for 10 minutes, then add the cabbage, mushrooms and fried tofu, and cover with a lid that fits inside the pan to keep everything submerged. Cook for another 5 minutes or so, until the cabbage is just tender. Bring to the boil and add the mangetout and cook for a further 2 minutes, then remove from the heat.

Divide the vegetables into 4 bowls and ladle over the dashi. Serve with a tiny bit of hot mustard on the side, as a dip for the vegetables or to be stirred directly into the broth.

DIFFICULTY
Not difficult times infinity, no takebacks!!!

SHIITAKE, ONION AND POTATO STEW
('SHIITAKE-JAGA')

SERVES 4

The meaty original version of this dish is called *nikujaga*, which translates as 'meat potato', a name I love for its stark, no-nonsense functionality. So I've called this dish 'shiitake-jaga', or 'shiitake potato', because that's what it is – a Japanese stew full of satisfying mushrooms and spuds, flavoured with the sulphuric sweetness of onions.

1 tablespoon oil
1 large or 2 small onions, thinly sliced
2 carrots, peeled and cut into wedges
2 large baking potatoes, peeled and cut into wedges
1 leek, washed and trimmed, cut into 4 pieces at
    an angle
400 g (14 oz) fresh shiitake mushrooms, destemmed
800 ml (27 fl oz/scant 3½ cups) dashi, ideally
    Mushroom Dashi (page 34)
4 tablespoons mirin
4 tablespoons soy sauce
1 tablespoon mushroom ketchup
2 tablespoons sake
100 g (3½ oz) mangetout (snow peas)
cooked rice, to serve

Heat the oil in a saucepan over a medium heat and fry the onions until just starting to soften, then add all the vegetables except the mangetout. Add the dashi, mirin, soy sauce, mushroom ketchup and sake and bring to a high simmer, then cover with a baking parchment cartouche or lid that fits inside the pan and continue to simmer for 10–15 minutes, until all the vegetables are soft.

Remove the baking parchment or lid, add the mangetout and cook for 1 final minute, then remove from the heat.

Serve in bowls with rice on the side.

DIFFICULTY
Entirely not difficult

CAULIFLOWER KATSU CURRY

The 'katsu' in katsu curry refers to the breaded, fried thing that goes onto it, not to the curry itself – and that breaded, fried thing can be just about anything. So why not our old friend cauliflower, which can be just as juicy, flavourful and satisfying as any chicken breast? The combination of farty-sweet cauliflower and the mellow spice of Japanese curry is a perfect match.

1 very large cauliflower, cut into 4 large vertical slabs that hold together at their cores
60 g (2 oz/scant ½ cup) plain (all-purpose) flour
vegan egg replacer, equivalent to 4 eggs, prepared according to the manufacturers' instructions, or 1 x recipe quantity Batter for Breadcrumbing (page 46)
120–150 g (4–5 oz/2½–2¾ cups) panko breadcrumbs
oil, for shallow-frying
few pinches of salt
800 ml (27 fl oz/scant 3½ cups) dashi (any kind, pages 33–34) or seasoned vegetable broth
200 g (7 oz) Japanese Curry Roux (page 49)
2 tablespoons soy sauce
2 tablespoons ketchup
hot chilli sauce, to taste
about 40 g (1½ oz) red pickled ginger, to garnish (optional)
few big pinches of sesame seeds, to garnish

Preheat the oven to 100°C (210°F/Gas ½).

Dredge the cauliflower slabs in the flour, then in the egg replacer or batter, and then in the panko, ensuring that they are completely and evenly coated.

Heat about 1 cm (½ in) depth of oil in a large frying pan (skillet) over a medium-high heat, then carefully lower in the cauliflower katsu and fry for about 5 minutes on each side, until golden brown all over. You will have to do this in batches unless you have an absolutely enormous frying pan, so drain the cauliflower on paper towels, season with a few pinches of salt, then place on a baking sheet and transfer to the oven to keep hot while the others are cooking.

Meanwhile, bring the dashi or broth to the boil in a saucepan and whisk in the curry roux, soy sauce, ketchup and hot sauce. Boil for another 5 minutes or so, whisking frequently, until the mixture thickens up nicely.

To serve, dish some rice up onto big plates, then ladle on the curry sauce and place the fried cauliflower on top (slice it first if you like, or just serve it with a knife and fork). Garnish with the pickled ginger, if using, and the sesame seeds.

DIFFICULTY
I'm gonna say... not difficult

STIR-FRIED CABBAGE AND BEAN SPROUTS WITH GINGER SAUCE

(KYABETSU TO MOYASHI NO SHŌGAYAKI)

SERVES 4

This dish is based on a Japanese soul food classic called *buta shōgayaki,* or pork stir-fried with ginger. But that dish is already about 50 per cent vegetables, maybe more, in the form of cabbage and bean sprouts. So I wondered, would it work without any pork at all? And it damn well does. The veg have a glorious crunch, and it's no less satisfying sans meat.

60 g (2 oz) fresh root ginger, peeled and thinly sliced
    against the grain
6 tablespoons soy sauce
6 tablespoons mirin
4 tablespoons sake
1 tablespoon ketchup
1 teaspoon sesame oil
1 tablespoon cornflour (cornstarch)
1 tablespoon vegetable oil
1 onion, finely sliced
1 hispi (pointed) cabbage, halved and cored,
    cut into strips about 1 cm (½ in) wide
300 g (10½ oz) bean sprouts
2 spring onions (scallions), finely sliced, to garnish
toasted white sesame seeds, to garnish
cooked rice, to serve

Purée the ginger, soy sauce, mirin, sake, ketchup, sesame oil and cornflour in a blender or food processor.

Heat the oil in a wok or deep frying pan (skillet) over a high heat and add the onion and cabbage. Stir-fry for 4–5 minutes, then add the bean sprouts and the ginger sauce. Keep stir-frying until the sprouts have softened slightly and the sauce has coated everything nicely, 3–4 minutes.

Garnish with spring onions and sesame seeds, and serve with rice.

DIFFICULTY
So not difficult I could plotz

JAPANESE-STYLE CELERIAC STEAK
(WAFŪ SERORIAKKU SUTĒKI)

I am in two minds regarding the phenomenon of calling vegetables cut into large slabs and cooked in a pan 'steaks'. I mean, on the one hand, they're not steaks. But on the other hand, who cares? So yes: two minds. Please subscribe to my podcast. But seriously, these pan-fried, slightly caramelised celeriac slabs, bathed in a sweet onion sauce and garnished with fried garlic, are so delicious, it really doesn't matter what you call them.

4 garlic cloves, thinly sliced
2 tablespoons vegetable oil
1 celeriac (celery root), peeled and cut into 3 big
   slabs, about 2.5 cm (1 in) thick
black pepper, to taste
1 teaspoon sesame oil
180–200 ml (6–7 fl oz/¾–scant 1 cup) Wafu Dressing
   (page 53)
few pinches of sesame seeds
½ punnet salad cress
2 spring onions (scallions), finely sliced

Place the garlic in a frying pan (skillet) with the cold oil and set over a medium heat. Allow the garlic to slowly fry in the oil until just golden brown, then remove with a slotted spoon and drain on paper towels.

Return the oil to the heat and turn it up to high, then lay the celeriac slabs in the oil and hit them with a few good grinds of black pepper. Cook on each side for about 5 minutes, until nicely browned (and perhaps starting to blacken in places), then drizzle over the sesame oil and the wafu dressing and let it boil briefly.

Remove from the heat, transfer the celeriac to a cutting board and slice it like a steak, then serve on warmed plates (yes! do it!) and pour over the sauce. Garnish with the sesame seeds, cress, spring onions and fried garlic.

DIFFICULTY
I still find it difficult to call a vegetable a 'steak', but I don't find it
difficult to cook or enjoy this dish

BIG RICE &

ご飯物と麺類

NOODLE DISHES

These dishes are meals in themselves
because they're quite voluminous and
already contain rice or noodles –
they're the Japanese equivalent of
a bowl of pasta: similarly filling,
simple and comfortingly carby.

SURPRISINGLY AWESOME ONE-HOUR SPICY SESAME, AUBERGINE AND COURGETTE RAMEN

SERVES 4

Ramen is a bit like marriage; you know it's going to take a long time, but nobody tells you it never ends until it's too late. None of the previous sentence makes sense, but then neither does this recipe: a ramen that defies ramen logic by being very delicious despite also being so many things that ramen is not supposed to be: fast, simple, vegan and based on a broth that's nothing special. This is achieved primarily through copious amounts of fat: particularly in the oil used to cook the veg, and in the tahini used to enrich the broth. It's the perfect recipe to make if you need to convince anybody that not all Japanese food, nor all vegan food, is light and healthy.

3 courgettes (zucchini)
3 tablespoons vinegar
1 teaspoon caster (superfine) or granulated (raw) sugar
pinch of salt
1 tablespoon chilli flakes, plus an extra pinch
1 big aubergine (eggplant)
4 tablespoons vegetable oil
4 tablespoons sesame oil
1½ teaspoons Sichuan pepper
4 garlic cloves, minced (ground)
1 cm (½ in) piece of fresh root ginger, peeled and minced (ground) or grated (shredded)
4 tablespoons soy sauce
2 tablespoons mirin
hot chilli sauce, to taste (optional)
1.2 litres (40 fl oz/4¾ cups) dashi, ideally Mushroom Dashi (page 34)
100 g (3½ oz) tahini
100 g (3½ oz) miso
¼ Chinese cabbage or similar cabbage, roughly chopped
4 portions of uncooked ramen noodles
4 tablespoons toasted sesame seeds, crushed to a coarse powder
1 spring onion (scallion), finely sliced

Cut half of one of the courgettes into long, thin matchsticks, or, if you have a spiraliser, bust it out and shred it into thin strands. Toss the shredded courgette with the vinegar, sugar, salt and pinch of chilli and leave to marinate while you prepare everything else.

Cut the remaining courgettes and the aubergine into wedges, about 1 cm (½ in) thick. Heat the vegetable oil, sesame oil, Sichuan pepper, garlic, ginger and 1 tablespoon chilli flakes together in a wide pan over a medium heat. Once it's hot, let everything sizzle for a few minutes, then add the courgette and aubergine wedges, stirring to coat them in the oil. Place a lid on the pan and let them steam-fry, stirring every couple of minutes or so, until the vegetables are very soft, about 15 minutes. Add the soy sauce and mirin, taste, and add chilli sauce if you want it spicier. Leave to cook for another 5 minutes or so for the veg to absorb the seasoning.

Meanwhile, bring the dashi to a low boil and whisk in the tahini and miso, ensuring that no lumps remain (if you have a hand-held stick blender, it's a good idea to use it). Reduce the seasoned broth to a simmer.

Bring a large pan of water to a rolling boil, and boil the cabbage for 1 minute, until just tender. Remove with a slotted spoon and reserve.

Let the water come back to the boil and cook the ramen until al dente, according to the packet instructions. Drain very well.

Divide the ramen among 4 deep bowls, pour over the miso-sesame broth and toss the noodles through the broth to ensure they aren't sticking together. Top with the aubergine and courgette mix (plus all of the oil), the crushed sesame, the pickled courgette, and the spring onion. Eat immediately and don't forget to slurp!

DIFFICULTY

As I was writing this, the cat knocked over one of my plants and the wet dirt got everywhere and this is a hell of a lot easier than cleaning that up

'RAMEN FOR FAYE WONG'
(MUSHROOM DASHI RAMEN WITH VEGETABLES AND FRIED TOFU)

SERVES 4

When I first opened Nanban, we had no vegetarian ramen on the menu. This is because I just thought vegetarian ramen was *wrong*. It's a meat dish and that's that – in Japan it's even sometimes called *nikusoba* – 'meat soba'. To make a veggie version seemed like a betrayal of what ramen is all about. But I gathered that the front of house staff were tired of having to explain why we didn't do a veggie ramen, so I gave it a go.

This is what I came up with, and it's delicious. We decided to name it after a vegetarian celebrity as they do with sandwiches in American delis, and eventually settled on Faye Wong, the Cantonese pop star/actor who was once named the world's sexiest vegetarian.

1 pack (300–350 g/10½–12 oz) firm silken tofu,
    cut into 8 rectangles
2 tablespoons sake
100 g (3½ oz/1 cup) cornflour (cornstarch)
1 tablespoon black sesame seeds
100 ml (3½ fl oz/scant ½ cup) plus 2 tablespoons
    vegetable oil
1 sheet of nori, or 1 tablespoon aonori flakes
big pinch of salt
1.2 litres (40 fl oz/4¾ cups) Mushroom Dashi
    (page 34)
90 ml (6 tablespoons) soy sauce
4 tablespoons mirin
about ½ daikon/mooli, peeled and cut into rounds
    about 2.5 cm (1 in) thick
80–100 g (3–3½ oz) enoki or shimeji mushrooms,
    roots removed and broken into small clusters
¼ Chinese cabbage, cut into 2.5 cm (1 in) strips
4 portions of uncooked ramen noodles
4 shiitake mushrooms (this is a good use for the
    rehydrated ones from making dashi), destemmed
    and thinly sliced
2 spring onions (scallions), finely sliced
½ mild red chilli, deseeded and very thinly grated
    (shredded)
a few strips of lemon or yuzu zest

Put the tofu into a small bowl and pour the sake over the tofu. Mix together the cornflour and sesame seeds, then carefully dredge the tofu in the cornflour mixture, ensuring it is evenly coated.

Heat the 2 tablespoons of oil in a non-stick frying pan (skillet) over a medium-high heat and cook for a few minutes on each side, until the tofu is golden brown and crisp. Drain on paper towels and set aside.

Purée the 100 ml (3½ fl oz/scant ½ cup) oil, nori and salt together in a food processor until the seaweed is completely pulverised. Leave the oil to settle while you prepare the rest of the dish.

Bring the dashi, soy sauce and mirin to the boil in a saucepan, then add the daikon rounds. Reduce the heat to a high simmer, place a lid on the pan and cook until the daikon are tender, about 10 minutes. Remove the daikon with a slotted spoon and reserve. If you're using shimeji mushrooms, boil them in the dashi for a couple of minutes, then remove and reserve (the enoki don't need cooking). Keep the dashi at a low simmer with a lid on the pan.

Bring a large pan of water to the boil and blanch the cabbage for 1 minute, then remove with a slotted spoon and reserve.

Let the water come back to the boil and cook the ramen until al dente, according to the packet instructions. Drain very well.

Divide the ramen among 4 deep bowls, pour over the mushroom dashi and toss the noodles with chopsticks to ensure they aren't stuck together. Top with the cabbage, daikon, mushrooms, tofu, spring onions, chilli shreds and lemon or yuzu zest. Finally, add a generous spoonful or two of the nori oil to the surface of the broth. Enjoy immediately, while watching *Chungking Express*, my favourite Faye Wong film.

DIFFICULTY

Beautifully not difficult

FRENCH ONION RAMEN

I can never figure out why French onion soup ever went out of style. It's just so good. I had some that my great aunt Jean made a few years back at a family get-together in Wisconsin and it made me think, 'I should eat French onion soup *every day!*'

Suddenly fixated on French onion soup, my thoughts quickly turned to ramen. The molten onions mingle beautifully with the noodles so you get a lovely sweetness and silky texture in every bite, all bathed in a rich, beefy broth that just happens to contain no beef. The onions do take a while to caramelise properly, but for comfort food I think it's worth the wait.

4 tablespoons olive oil
2 red onions, halved and thinly sliced
2 brown onions, halved and thinly sliced
pinch of salt, or more, to taste
1 teaspoon caster (superfine) or granulated (raw) sugar
2 garlic cloves, crushed and thinly sliced
4 tablespoons sake
2 tablespoons ruby port or red wine
1.2 litres (40 fl oz/4¾ cups) Mushroom or Triple Seaweed Dashi (page 34)
2 bay leaves
4 sprigs of fresh thyme (optional)
a few grinds of black pepper, or more, to taste
4 tablespoons soy sauce, or more, to taste
1 tablespoon balsamic vinegar
1 tablespoon mirin, or more, to taste
1 tablespoon Marmite (yeast extract)
1½ teaspoons cornflour (cornstarch)
200 g (7 oz) fresh spinach, washed
¼ Savoy cabbage, cut into thin strips
4 portions of uncooked ramen noodles
4 spring onions (scallions), thinly sliced
80 g (3 oz) bamboo shoots (if you can, use Japanese menma – pickled bamboo shoots)
a few drops of sesame oil and/or truffle oil
60–80 g (2–3 oz) vegan cheese ('Cheddar' or 'Italian-style'), grated (shredded)
4 slices of good-quality bread, toasted

Heat the oil in a deep saucepan or casserole (Dutch oven) and add the onions and the salt. Cook over a medium-high heat for 10 minutes or so, stirring frequently, until they soften, then reduce the heat to medium-low and cook for another 45–50 minutes, stirring every 10 minutes. After about 15 minutes, the onions will start to caramelise, so make sure you scrape the bottom of the pan when you stir to prevent them from catching and burning prematurely. When the onions are just starting to brown, stir in the sugar and add the garlic. During the last 10 minutes of cooking, you will have to stir and scrape often to ensure the onions don't burn. (If it's proving difficult to scrape up the stuck bits, add a splash of water, which should help them release nicely.)

Add the sake and the port or wine. Add the dashi, bay leaves, thyme and black pepper and bring to a simmer. Simmer for 30 minutes, then stir in the soy sauce, balsamic vinegar, mirin and Marmite. Taste and adjust the seasoning as you like it – it should be fairly salty and slightly sweet. Remove the bay leaves and thyme stems and discard. Spoon about 3 tablespoons of the broth into a small dish and leave to cool. Stir the cornflour into the cooled broth to make a thin slurry, then stir it back into the soup and bring to the boil to thicken the broth slightly.

Bring a large saucepan full of water to the boil and blanch the spinach for 15 seconds. Remove with a slotted spoon and rinse under cold water. Drain well, pressing out any excess water. In the same pan, boil the cabbage for 3–4 minutes until just tender, then remove with a slotted spoon and set aside.

Let the water return to a rolling boil, then cook the ramen until al dente, according to the packet instructions. Drain well.

Divide the ramen among 4 deep bowls and ladle over the soup. Gently stir the noodles through the soup to ensure they aren't sticking together. Top each ramen with the spinach, cabbage, spring onions, bamboo shoots, sesame or truffle oil and vegan cheese. Serve with the toast on the side to soak up the broth once the noodles have all been slurped away.

DIFFICULTY

So not difficult it will make you weep

CURRY RAMEN

The noodle most commonly paired with curry in Japan is udon, which is nice, but personally I'd like to see a lot more curry ramen, starting with this one. I think the viscosity of Japanese curry broth makes it a natural partner for ramen, which is usually served with meaty broths that have a lot of body from fat and collagen. But to be honest you can use whatever noodle you like here – it's not exactly a 'traditional' dish, so you won't run afoul of the Japanese Culinary Authenticity Police if you make it with udon or somen instead of ramen.

1.2 litres (40 fl oz/4¾ cups) dashi (any kind, pages 33–34) or seasoned vegetable broth
200 g (7 oz) Japanese Curry Roux (page 49)
3–4 tablespoons soy sauce (to taste)
hot chilli sauce, to taste
100 g (3½ oz) fresh spinach
½ hispi (pointed) cabbage, cut into strips about 1 cm (½ in) wide
150 g (5 oz) bean sprouts
4 portions of uncooked ramen noodles
4 spring onions (scallions), finely sliced
a few big pinches of sesame seeds
about 60 g (2 oz) red pickled ginger
a few spoonfuls of chilli oil or sesame oil (to taste)

Bring the dashi or broth to the boil and whisk in the curry roux, soy sauce and chilli sauce. Let the mixture boil for a few minutes until it thickens up nicely, then reduce to a low simmer, drop in the spinach, and place a lid on the pan.

Bring a large pot of water to the boil and blanch the cabbage and bean sprouts for 1–2 minutes, then remove with a slotted spoon or a sieve (fine-mesh strainer) and reserve.

Let the water come back up to a rolling boil, then cook the ramen until al dente, according to the packet instructions. Drain well.

Divide the ramen among 4 deep bowls and ladle over the soup and spinach. Use chopsticks to gently stir the noodles through the soup, then top with the cabbage and bean sprouts, spring onions, sesame seeds, pickled ginger and chilli or sesame oil.

DIFFICULTY
Excessively not difficult

RAMEN SALAD
(HIYASHI CHŪKA)

SERVES 4

Summers in most of the Japanese archipelago are brutally hot and humid, hardly conducive to ramen eating, which is the culinary equivalent of sitting in a steam room. So ramen shops in Japan usually offer something like this chilled ramen salad, called *hiyashi chūka,* to get the customers in. The noodles ensure it's a substantial meal, but it's still light and fresh.

100 g (3½ oz) cherry tomatoes, halved
1 tablespoon soy sauce
2 teaspoons caster (superfine) or granulated (raw) sugar
1 teaspoon sesame oil
100 g (3½ oz) mixed salad leaves – try to get a mix of peppery/mild and crunchy/tender – I like pea shoots and rocket (arugula)
½ cucumber, julienned
2 carrots, peeled and julienned
4 portions of uncooked ramen noodles
240 ml (8½ fl oz/1 cup) Sesame Dressing (page 42), thinned with a little water and salt or soy sauce, or 240 ml (8½ fl oz/1 cup) Wafu Dressing (page 53)
2 avocados, sliced about 3 mm (⅛ in) thick
a few pinches of sesame seeds

Preheat the oven to 180°C (350°F/Gas 6).

Toss the cherry tomatoes together with the soy sauce, sugar and sesame oil, then transfer to a baking sheet and bake for 20 minutes, until they're slightly shrivelled and browned. Leave them to cool, then toss them together with the salad leaves, cucumber and carrots.

Bring a large pan of water to a rolling boil. Cook the ramen a little more than al dente (the noodles firm up a lot when you chill them down), then drain and rinse very well under cold running water – they should be thoroughly chilled, with as little excess starch as possible. Drain well, then toss with the dressing of your choice.

Transfer to plates or shallow bowls, along with any dressing left in the bowl, then top with the salad mixture, avocado slices and sesame seeds.

DIFFICULTY

Deliciously not difficult

CHILLED SOBA WITH TSUYU
(ZARU SOBA)

SERVES 4

This exquisitely simple dish is one of my all-time favourites: almost entirely unadorned soba noodles, served chilled with a flavourful tsuyu for dipping. Soba are one of the rare noodles that taste great all on their own, because of the rich, nutty flavour of buckwheat. When you're shopping for soba, try to find ones that are 100 per cent buckwheat. They're a little bit hard to come by, but the flavour is fantastic, with a sweet, fragrant aroma that almost reminds me of cocoa. (A zaru, by the way, is a kind of bamboo sieve (strainer), on which these noodles are traditionally served.)

This is quite a light dish, which is fine if you aren't that hungry, but if you want to make the meal more substantial, Tempura (page 118) is a good choice for a side dish, because you can use the same tsuyu for the dip.

4 portions of uncooked soba noodles
1 x recipe quantity Vegan Tsuyu (page 37)
½ sheet of nori, snipped into fine shreds
   with scissors
2 spring onions (scallions), finely sliced
a tiny bit of wasabi (optional)

Cook the soba until al dente, according to the packet instructions – I'd recommend boiling them until they're slightly undercooked, then switching off the heat and letting them sit in the hot water for a couple of minutes, which I think yields a slightly less brittle, more flexible noodle. Drain and rinse the noodles very well under cold running water, until they are completely chilled and there is no excess starch on them.

Transfer to plates and top with the nori. Put the tsuyu into a cup on the side. Place the spring onions in the tsuyu and serve the wasabi in another dish on the side, to be mixed in as you like.

DIFFICULTY
Joyously not difficult

YAKISOBA

SERVES 4

I've always found it weird how some Japanese dishes seem to engender intense obsession among both chefs and diners, while others don't. Sushi chefs are known for their extreme discipline, craftsmanship and attention to detail, and their devotees are similarly discriminating to a degree that would terrify most chefs, particularly in our current era of TripAdvisor and Yelp. Ramen gets the same kind of treatment – ramen chefs are increasingly thoughtful and precise to satisfy increasingly discerning and demanding customers. I've even recently come across Instagram accounts devoted to documenting and evaluating the best *potato salads* in Tokyo.

But what of *yakisoba*, the delightful but often overlooked stir-fried noodle dish? It doesn't seem to get much love – I guess it's because it's considered quite simple, really, something just about anybody could make. But that doesn't mean it can't be just as delicious as more fussed-over dishes; in fact, great yakisoba is a thing of beauty. Maybe someday not too far in the future we'll even have a Michelin-starred yakisoba shop. Until then... here's a pretty damn good recipe.

2 tablespoons oil
2 onions, sliced about 5 mm (¼ in) thick
2 carrots, peeled and halved, then cut at an angle
    into strips about 2 mm thick
½ hispi (pointed) cabbage, cut into 1 cm (½ in) strips
6 shiitake mushrooms, destemmed and thinly sliced
1 tablespoon sesame oil
½ teaspoon dashi powder
3 tablespoons soy sauce
2 tablespoons ketchup
2 tablespoons mirin
1 tablespoon sake
1 tablespoon mushroom ketchup
big pinch of white pepper
4 portions of cooked ramen noodles or similar
    Chinese wheat noodles
1 tablespoon toasted white sesame seeds
40–50 g (1½–2 oz) red pickled ginger
2 spring onions (scallions), thinly sliced
½ sheet nori, snipped into fine shreds with
    scissors (optional)

Heat the oil in a wok or a big frying pan (skillet) over a high heat, add the onions and fry for a few minutes, until they are beginning to colour. Add the carrots, cabbage and mushrooms and fry for another few minutes, then add the sesame oil, dashi powder, soy sauce, ketchup, mirin, sake, mushroom ketchup and white pepper. Let the liquid reduce slightly, then add the noodles and sesame seeds. Cook for a few more minutes to let the noodles soak up the sauce.

Serve in bowls, topped with the pickled ginger, spring onions and nori. You may also enjoy this topped with a tiny bit of hot mustard, or a drizzle of Vegan Japanese Mayo (page 43).

DIFFICULTY
So not difficult I just can't even

PESTO UDON

SERVES 4

Recently, there's been a bit of a trend in Japan, and at Japanese restaurants abroad, for 'carbonara udon', which plays on the Japanese tradition of mixing raw egg into udon by simply adding varying degrees of other carbonara elements, namely Parmesan cheese, bacon and black pepper. But why stop there? Udon is similar to chunky Italian pastas like pici, bucatini and linguini, so it works well with any kind of sauce or topping that works with them, including lovely pesto, which seemed to be really popular in the 1990s, but has since gone out of fashion. I reckon it's time for a pesto revival, starting with pesto udon.

50 g (2 oz) pine nuts
1 garlic clove, finely grated
70–80 g (2¾–3 oz) basil leaves
50 g (2 oz) white miso or vegan
    'Parmesan-style' cheese
120 ml (4 fl oz/½ cup) olive oil
4 portions of udon noodles
freshly cracked black pepper

Preheat the oven to 180°C (350°F/Gas 6).
    Place the pine nuts on a baking sheet and roast for 5 minutes. If they're golden brown, take them out, but if not, keep roasting for another few minutes (they can go from nicely browned to burnt very quickly, so keep your eye on them). You can also toast them in a frying pan (skillet), but I find this gives them a really uneven colour. Remove from the oven and leave to cool.
    Transfer the nuts to a food processor or mortar with the garlic, basil and white miso or cheese (reserve a few pine nuts and basil leaves for the garnish), and pound or process until broken down, then add the oil and continue to blend until smooth.
    Cook the udon according to the packet instructions. Drain, then return the noodles to the pan and add the sauce, tossing the noodles to coat them well.
    Serve in pasta bowls, topped with a few leaves of torn basil, a few pine nuts and a twist of black pepper.

NOTE This uses a recipe for a vegan pesto sauce, but if there's a brand of jarred vegan pesto sauce you like, by all means just use that!

DIFFICULTY
It is difficult to stop eating this, but it is not difficult to make

ご飯物と麺類   156   BIG RICE & NOODLE DISHES

ICED SUMMER SOMEN WITH LEMON

SERVES 4

Everybody knows ramen, soba and udon – the Holy Trinity of Japanese noodles – but how about somen? Somen, extremely thin and delicate wheat noodles, are actually one of my favourite noodles, although that's partly to do with memories of a certain way of serving them called *nagashi somen*. Nagashi means 'flowing', and that's exactly what they are – cooked, chilled somen are sent down a stream of flowing water in a bamboo chute in front of guests, who then pluck the noodles out with chopsticks as they rush by. They then dip the noodles in a cup of tsuyu and slurp them up, then wait for the next noodles to float on down for their next mouthful. It's ridiculous, but it's a hell of a lot of fun, and so refreshing in the summer – even the sound of the flowing water has a cooling effect. But you don't need to bust out your bamboo and your garden hose to enjoy somen – this recipe will do nicely just as it is. Enjoy on the hottest day of the year, or whenever you need some noodle-y refreshment.

1 lemon
1 litre (34 fl oz/4 cups) dashi, ideally Kombu or Triple
    Seaweed Dashi (pages 33–34)
4 tablespoons soy sauce
1 tablespoon mirin
½ cucumber, deseeded and julienned
½ green apple or Asian pear, cored and julienned
50 g (2 oz) radishes, thinly sliced (use a mandoline
    if you have one)
2 spring onions (scallions), finely sliced
a handful of pea shoots
1 cm (½ in) piece of fresh root ginger, peeled and
    finely grated (shredded)
4 portions of uncooked somen noodles
1 tablespoon sesame seeds
1 teaspoon sesame oil

Peel the lemon with a vegetable peeler, making sure not to leave too much white pith on the peel. Twist the lemon peels over the dashi to infuse it with their oils, then add the peels to the dashi along with the soy sauce, mirin and the juice of the lemon. Transfer to the freezer while you prepare the other ingredients – the dashi should be semi-frozen, not quite like a slush but more like a lake with a thin layer of ice on it in the winter. It should take about 30 minutes, perhaps a bit longer. Once it's starting to freeze, remove the lemon peels and discard.

Meanwhile, prepare the vegetables.

Cook the somen in boiling water according to the packet instructions – cooking should be very brief, about 1 minute or even less. Drain the somen and rinse under plenty of cold running water to stop the cooking and get rid of excess starch.

Divide the noodles among 4 shallow bowls and pour over the semi-frozen dashi, using chopsticks to gently toss the noodles through the soup. Top each bowl with the vegetables, the pea shoots, sesame seeds and a few drops of sesame oil.

DIFFICULTY
Refreshingly not difficult

PORTOBELLO MUSHROOM AND ONION 'SUKIYAKI' BOWL

SERVES 4

This recipe is a sort of combination of two noble Japanese beef dishes: *sukiyaki* (beef hotpot) and *gyūdon* (beef bowl). Both feature a sweetened soy-based sauce, and I think gyūdon is particularly nice because it also uses a lot of semi-caramelised onions, like the kind you get from hot dog stands. And between the sauce and onions, there's so much flavour here you hardly need the beef, but eating a bowl of saucy onions on rice seems odd, so I've replaced the beef with nice, meaty portobello mushrooms.

2 tablespoons oil
4 onions, thinly sliced
8 very large portobello mushrooms
  (about 500 g/1 lb 2 oz), cut into chunks no wider
  than 1 cm (½ in)
2 cm (¾ in) piece of fresh root ginger, peeled and
  finely julienned
100 ml (3½ fl oz/scant ½ cup) Sweet Soy Sauce
  (page 40)
100 ml (3½ fl oz/scant ½ cup) dashi, ideally
  Mushroom Dashi (page 34)
4 large portions of cooked rice (350–400 g/
  12–14 oz/1¾–2 cups uncooked weight)
2 spring onions (scallions), thinly sliced
40–50 g (1½–2 oz) red pickled ginger
toasted white sesame seeds, to garnish

Heat the oil in a large frying pan (skillet) over a medium heat, add the onions and cook until they are soft and brown, then add the mushrooms and ginger. Let the mushrooms brown a bit, then add the sweet soy and dashi, bring it to the boil and let it reduce slightly, to the consistency of a thin syrup.

Spoon the mushrooms and onions, along with the sauce, over cooked rice in deep bowls, and garnish with the spring onions, pickled ginger and sesame seeds.

DIFFICULTY
Where's the 'not difficult' emoji?

'CHANPON' STIR-FRIED VEGETABLE BOWL

SERVES 4

Chanpon is a dish from Nagasaki that is often thought to be a kind of proto-ramen: a jumble of vegetables (and usually seafood, and sometimes meat) boiled or stir-fried, then set atop pudgy alkaline wheat noodles in a medium-bodied broth. Invented by Chinese expats in the late 19th century, it was ramen before ramen was called ramen. The origins of the word 'chanpon' itself aren't quite clear, but now it is taken to mean a 'mixture' or 'hodgepodge'. This dish isn't quite chanpon, because it's got a sauce rather than a broth (so this works on rice as well as noodles), but the spirit is there – chanpon can be many things, but it is always generous, hearty and colourful. And that's exactly what this is.

2 tablespoons vegetable oil
1 onion, thinly sliced
2 carrots, halved and thinly sliced at an angle
6 shiitake mushrooms (fresh or rehydrated from dried), destemmed and sliced
8 garlic cloves, thinly sliced
1 hispi (pointed) cabbage, quartered and coarsely chopped
300 g (10½ oz) bean sprouts
2 spring onions (scallions), coarsely chopped
250 ml (8½ fl oz/1 cup) dashi (any kind, pages 33–34)
1½ tablespoons cornflour (cornstarch)
4 tablespoons sake
2 tablespoons soy sauce
1 tablespoon sesame oil
big pinch of salt, or to taste
¼ teaspoon white pepper
100 g (3½ oz) mangetout (snow peas)
50–60 g (2 oz) red pickled ginger
4 portions of uncooked ramen or similar wheat noodles, or 4 large portions of cooked rice (400 g/14 oz/2 cups uncooked weight)

Heat the vegetable oil in a large frying pan (skillet) or wok over a high heat. Add the onion and carrots and stir-fry for a few minutes until they soften slightly and the onions start to become translucent. Add the mushrooms, garlic and cabbage and continue to stir-fry for about 5 minutes, until the cabbage has wilted slightly, then add the bean sprouts and spring onions.

Combine a little bit of the dashi with the cornflour and stir together to make a thin slurry. Add the remaining dashi, sake, soy sauce, sesame oil, a big pinch of salt and the white pepper to the pan and bring to the boil, then pour in the cornflour mixture and continue to stir-fry until the sauce thickens, about 5 minutes. Add the mangetout and pickled ginger and cook for another 1 minute, then taste and add salt as needed.

Cook the noodles (if using) according to the packet instructions, then divide the noodles or rice into 4 deep bowls and top with the stir-fry and sauce.

DIFFICULTY

Not difficult forever

'FRIDGE DRAWER' FRIED RICE

SERVES 4

Fried rice was one of the first things I ever learned to cook. That's partly because fried rice was one of my favourite foods growing up, but also because it's just so easy. And also because it will kind of take anything – there are, I suppose, things that *don't* taste good in fried rice, but I'm struggling to think of any right now. Chocolate frosting, I guess. Alright, let me backtrack a bit – fried rice will take any *vegetable*, and that includes ones you might not expect, like lettuce, cucumber or beetroot (beets). That's why I call this 'fridge drawer' fried rice – just use whatever's in there.

2 tablespoons oil
1 onion, finely diced
4 garlic cloves, finely chopped
a couple handfuls of vegetables – any veg –
    very finely diced (no bigger than 5 mm/⅛ in);
    a few of my favourites are carrots, mushrooms,
    asparagus, tenderstem broccoli and courgette
    (zucchini)
4 large portions of cooked rice (350–400 g/
    12–14 oz/1¾–2 cups uncooked weight),
    ideally from the day before
3 tablespoons soy sauce
1 tablespoon sesame oil
1½ tablespoons mirin
¼ teaspoon dashi powder
4 spring onions (scallions), roughly chopped
50 g (2 oz) red pickled ginger (optional)
white or black pepper, to taste
1 teaspoon toasted white sesame seeds

Heat the oil in a frying pan (skillet) or wok over a high heat, add the onion and stir-fry until translucent and beginning to brown. Add the garlic and all the other vegetables, and stir-fry for about 5 minutes, until the veg are cooked through, then add the rice, soy sauce, sesame oil, mirin and dashi powder. Break up the rice with a wooden spoon or spatula as you stir-fry, ensuring that there are no clumps. When the rice has absorbed all the liquid in the pan, add the spring onions, pickled ginger, pepper and white sesame seeds.
    Serve in shallow bowls.

DIFFICULTY
Sincerely not difficult

MIXED VEGETABLE RICE
(TAKIKOMI GOHAN)

This hearty one-pot pilaf-ish rice dish is usually served as a side, but I think it's got enough going on in terms of flavour, texture and substance that it can be a meal on its own. It's made with all sorts of veg – traditionally five different ones, but it can be any number. I like veg that provide a range of colours as well as flavours, but go ahead and use whatever you have on hand.

300 g (10½ oz/1½ cups) rice, washed
400 ml (13 fl oz/generous 1½ cups) dashi (any kind, pages 33–34)
2 tablespoons soy sauce
1 tablespoon mirin
1 tablespoon sake
½ carrot, peeled and finely diced
1 small turnip, peeled and finely diced
small handful (about 80 g/3 oz) mushrooms (shiitake or shimeji are my favourite), destemmed and cut or torn into bite-size chunks, if necessary
80 g (3 oz) frozen edamame beans (shelled) or peas
1 tablespoon dried wakame

Place the rice in a saucepan with a snug-fitting lid along with the dashi, soy sauce, mirin and sake. Place the prepared vegetables and wakame on top of the rice, set the pan over a high flame on a small burner and bring to the boil with the lid off. Place the lid on the pan, reduce the heat to very low, and steam for 15 minutes.

Remove from the heat and leave to sit, covered, for 5 minutes, then remove the lid and gently fold the vegetables through the rice.

DIFFICULTY
Only slightly more difficult than making plain rice, which, by the way, is not difficult

'PRIMAVERA' FRIED RICE

When I was growing up, all the Italian restaurants (except for the truly old-school red-sauce-only places) had something on their menu called 'pasta primavera'. This dish was invented in New York in the late 1970s, presumably utilising seasonal spring ingredients, but by the time it made it to Wisconsin, it seemed to be just a catch-all name for any pasta featuring green vegetables, even if those green vegetables were just broccoli and frozen peas. But it's still a nice name, so I've pilfered it for this light and fresh fried rice I make in the spring, when some of my all-time favourite vegetables are all in season, namely asparagus, peas and wild garlic.

2 tablespoons oil (olive oil is nice in this)
1 onion, finely diced
4 garlic cloves, finely chopped
2 cm (¾ in) piece of fresh root ginger, peeled and grated (shredded)
150–200 g (5–7 oz) peas (frozen are fine, but use fresh if they're in season)
1 bunch (about 150 g/5 oz) asparagus, woody ends removed and cut into 2.5 cm (1 in) chunks
4 large portions of cooked rice (350–400 g/ 12–14 oz/1¾–2 cups uncooked weight), ideally from the day before
big pinch of salt
1½ tablespoons mirin
¼ teaspoon dashi powder
zest and juice of ¼ lemon
4 spring onions (scallions), roughly chopped
white pepper, to taste
1 teaspoon toasted white sesame seeds
a big handful (40–50 g/1½–2 oz) wild garlic leaves, coarsely chopped (if you can't get wild garlic, add more chopped garlic and use spinach instead)

Heat the oil in a frying pan (skillet) or wok over a high heat, add the onion and stir-fry until translucent and beginning to brown. Add the garlic, ginger, peas and asparagus and stir-fry for about 5 minutes, until the veg are cooked through, then add the rice, salt, mirin, dashi powder, and lemon zest and juice. Break up the rice with a wooden spoon or spatula as you stir-fry, ensuring that there are no clumps. When the rice has absorbed all the liquid in the pan, add the spring onions, pepper and white sesame seeds. Cook for a few more minutes, then remove from the heat and stir through the wild garlic until wilted thoroughly.
Serve in shallow bowls.

DIFFICULTY

Primavery not difficult

ROUGH NIGHT RICE

SERVES 2, 3 IF YOU'RE FEELING GENEROUS,
1 IF YOU ARE REALLY VERY DRUNK AND GREEDY

Rice has always been one of my favourite things to eat when I'm blotto. This is mainly because, back in college, I lived in dorms without kitchens, and the only piece of equipment I owned was a rice cooker that was originally given to my parents as a wedding present back in 1979. So, after a night of partying, I'd stumble back to my room and cook some rice. It was ideal for cooking while drunk, because all I had to do was dump in rice and water and switch it on.

I still love rice when I'm pickled. However, after so many years in London I've also developed a fondness for drunken kebabs – all greasy and meaty to slow down the effects of the alcohol, but with tangy/spicy condiments and a bit of fresh veg to perk yourself up as well. A few years ago, I decided to combine rice and kebab-like flavours in what I'd hoped would be the perfect drinking food, called 'Rough Night Rice'. Not only is it really delicious and filling, it's also absurdly easy (it's all cooked ahead, then microwaved and garnished) so that even the bar staff could make it if we couldn't get a chef to stay late. So if you're planning a big night out, do yourself a favour and prep this earlier in the day – it'll take the edge off both the booze and its after-effects.

2 tablespoons oil
½ red onion, finely diced
4 garlic cloves, finely sliced
2 pak choi (bok choi)/¼ cabbage/handful of tender-
    stem broccoli or similar, roughly chopped
3 vegan sausages, chopped up
150 g (5 oz) Kimchi (page 56)
200 g (7 oz/generous 1 cup) rice (uncooked weight),
    cooked according to the instructions on page 26
a glug of soy sauce
a splash of mirin
2 tablespoons sesame seeds, crushed to a coarse
    powder
1 jalapeño, finely sliced (optional)
2 spring onions (scallions), finely sliced
¼ lime
a drizzle of hot chilli sauce
a drizzle of vegan mayo

BEFORE DRINKING

Heat the oil in a frying pan (skillet) or wok over a medium heat, add most of the onion (save a spoonful to use later as garnish) and stir-fry until translucent and beginning to brown. Add the garlic, greens and sausages and stir-fry for about 5 minutes, until the veg are tender and the sausages are browned. Add the kimchi and cook until the kimchi liquid has evaporated, then add the rice, soy sauce and mirin. Break up the rice with a wooden spoon or spatula as you stir-fry, add the sesame and work it through.

Remove from the heat, leave to cool, then pack into microwaveable containers.

Combine the reserved red onion, jalapeño, spring onions and lime wedge in a separate container. Keep the rice and the garnish in the refrigerator until you're drunk.

AFTER DRINKING

Open the lid on the rice a crack, and microwave for 3–4 minutes, until piping hot throughout.

Transfer to a bowl and drizzle over the hot sauce and mayo. Add the fresh garnishes to the top and squeeze over the lime. Give everything a good stir, before shovelling it into your face. Pass out on the couch.

WARNING: Do not attempt to cook this recipe, or anything else, while drunk.

DIFFICULTY
Intoxicatingly not difficult

VEGAN BENTO

DIFFICULTY You'll be the envy of your office mates, so worth doing
even if it is difficult (but it's not)

HOW TO MAKE LOVELY JAPANESE
LUNCHBOXES WITH MINIMAL EFFORT

Bento are Japanese lunchboxes that can range from
humdrum grab-and-go items found in convenience
stores all the way up to breathtakingly beautiful
miniature feasts served at special functions. Either
way, they're delicious, and it's not as hard to make
them on a regular basis as you might think. Although
they're known for containing a vast multitude of
preparations – and that is sometimes the case –
bento can be really simple, sometimes made up of
just rice and one other thing. But even if you want a
bit more variety than that, it's not very hard at all. It
just requires a little planning.

Let's tackle the simplest kind of bento first:
just rice (or, rarely, another carb) plus something
flavourful and substantial to go with it. Remember,
you'll probably be eating this cold, so it should be
something that won't be gross if it's not hot. A few
suggestions:

- Squash Braised in Dashi with Mirin
  and Ginger (page 71)
- Teriyaki-Roasted Carrots (page 72)
- Sweet Miso-Roasted Beetroot (page 78)
- Fried Baby Aubergine Soaked in Dashi
  (page 97)
- Tofu Patties (page 74)
- Stir-Fried Cabbage and Bean Sprouts
  with Ginger Sauce (page 136)

Since the bulk of this kind of bento is rice, you'll need
a good size portion of it – use 75–100 g (2½–3½ oz/
generous ⅓ cup–½ cup) uncooked rice per bento.
The servings provided in each recipe will be about
right for 1 bento as well (i.e., if a recipe says it serves
4, it will make about 4 of these simple bento).

By the way, you should get your bento out of the
refrigerator about 1 hour before lunchtime, if you
can – this will make the rice less hard. Alternatively,
you can make Sushi Rice (page 108) for your
bento, which stays softer. To make a slightly more
impressive bento – let's say 4 things, because that's

often the number of compartments you'll find in a
bento or a plastic container with divisions – add to

the rice and the 'main' 2 little salads or pickle-type
items, such as:

- Pickled Cabbage (page 56)
- Citrus-Pickled Radishes (page 57)
- Pimp Your Edamame (page 62)
- Kale with Crushed Sesame (page 67)
- Cucumber and Wakame with Seasoned
  Vinegar (page 86)
- Sweet Crunchy Vegetables Kinpira-Style
  (page 90)

For a bento of 4 little things like this, you'll only
need about 50 g (2 oz/¼ cup) rice (uncooked), plus
roughly half of each recipe serving – so if a recipe
provides 4 servings, it'll make about 8 bento.

The easiest way to make bento is to do them
all at once – I always make 4 each week, because
I stay at home with my daughter on Mondays and
can whip up a bunch of different things during the
day to have for the remainder of the week. I have 4
containers, each with 4 compartments, so I can put
them together assembly-line-style once everything
is made, and then I don't have to worry about it for
the rest of the week (pretty much everything in this
book will last 4–5 days in the refrigerator, by the way).
Play around with it to suit your lunchtime behaviours
– if you end up getting lunch out a lot because of
work or social obligations, then 4 or 5 bento will be
too many. My advice is to just make a lot of Japanese
food – a bit more than you know you'll need – on a
Sunday or Monday and then turn the leftovers into
as many bento as you can.

The other day, a friend of mine asked me, 'What is
a bento?' After some consideration, thinking back on
all the bento I've eaten, and how diverse they've all
been, I just said: 'It's Japanese food... in a box'.

So there you have it: if you want to eat bento, just
make Japanese food, and put it in a box! Truly, the
difference between leftovers in a Tupperware and
a lovely bento is just a matter of perspective.

DESSERTS

デザートと飲み物

& DRINKS

Often based on fruit and legumes rather than butter and cream, Japanese sweets are naturally suited to a plant-based diet. There are a few traditional recipes to try here, but also some of my own creations that aren't quite Japanese, but do incorporate Japanese flavours. And there are drinks, of course! To be enjoyed with a Japanese meal, or not – they're delicious and refreshing on any occasion.

RED BEAN AND CHESTNUT JELLY
(YŌKAN)

MAKES 8 BIG SLICES OR 16 LITTLE ONES

Azuki beans are a key ingredient in East Asian sweets, found in everything from bread rolls to shaved ice. Häagen-Dazs even sells a red bean ice cream in China, Korea and Japan. Many Westerners find this a bit odd at first, but honestly I don't think I know of anybody who hasn't come to love it. My wife says that when she was a little girl, her (Japanese) mother told her red bean paste was chocolate, a devilish lie that she believed until she was in school. And actually, it's not that far off – the beans have a similarly lush, fudgy texture and subtle nutty-fruity flavour. One of my favourite red bean preparations is one of the most classic: *yōkan* jelly, a very traditional sweet set with agar, with a texture kind of like *pâté de fruit*. Enjoy this as a snack with a cup of green tea, or as a light dessert.

1 × 400 g (14 oz) tin azuki beans, including the water
finely grated zest and juice of 1 clementine
200 g (7 oz/1 cup) light brown sugar
2 teaspoons powdered agar or 2 tablespoons agar flakes
100 g (3½ oz/¾ cup) cooked chestnuts, chopped

Combine the azuki beans and their water with the clementine zest and juice and the sugar in a saucepan. Bring to the boil and cook for 5–10 minutes to soften the beans, stirring freqently, then add the agar and use a hand-held stick blender or food processor to purée the mixture until smooth. Stir in the chestnuts, then pour into a rectangular container and refrigerate until set and thoroughly chilled, about 4 hours.

Tip out of the container and slice into rectangular slabs to serve. Stored in the refrigerator, this will keep for up to 1 week.

DIFFICULTY
I don't think you're ready for this not difficult jelly

CRUNCHY SHICHIMI CHOCOLATE CHUNKS

Maybe I shouldn't mention this in a vegan cookbook (my editor told me to 'tone down' the references to meat-eating*), but I once had the pleasure of cooking a nose-to-tail pork dinner for my friend Jay Rayner, probably the best food critic in the country, and certainly the most enthusiastic. Jay is perhaps best known for his scathing takedowns of awful restaurants and hapless MasterChef contestants alike (in fact, he has published two books compiling his most hilariously brutal reviews), but in real life he is a warm-hearted and generous *bon vivant* who primarily just wants to have a nice time, and wants those around him to have a nice time as well. So for him I pulled out all the stops, cooking a (frankly insane) 15-course pork feast, and I even managed to include some pig in one of the desserts: chunks of dark chocolate with a sprinkle of shichimi chilli powder and bits of crunchy pork rind for texture. They were surprisingly tasty – the fact that they didn't taste much of pork was probably a good thing, and the real revelation was the combination of shichimi and chocolate. I've always enjoyed chilli and chocolate, but shichimi also contains orange zest, sesame and ginger, all of which are delicious with chocolate as well. For crunch, you can use either vegan cornflakes or rice crackers, which are honestly an improvement on the pork skin, and a lot easier to prepare.

a block of dark chocolate, chopped
a little handful of cornflakes or plain rice crackers, crushed
a pinch or two of shichimi
a little pinch of sea salt

Melt the chocolate in a heatproof bowl set over a pan of simmering water, or in the microwave in 20–30-second bursts. Stir in the cornflakes or rice crackers, then tip out onto a tray or plate lined with baking parchment and spread out into a thin layer. Sprinkle over the shichimi and sea salt, then chill in the refrigerator until completely set. Break into chunks to serve.

* Sorry Kate!

DIFFICULTY
This recipe is so not difficult it doesn't even have measurements

ALMOND JELLY WITH MANGO AND BROWN SUGAR SYRUP
(ANNIN DŌFU)

SERVES 4

This is a Chinese dessert that is also popular in Japan, kind of like a blancmange or panna cotta, but more delicate, easier to make and completely vegan. In China and Japan, it's traditionally made from apricot kernel milk or apricot kernel powder, which I've never seen in any shops, apparently it also contains small amounts of cyanide... so let's go with almond milk, which is kind of similar. The barely-set texture is like crème caramel or silken tofu – hence its Japanese name, *annin dōfu* (apricot kernel tofu). It is exceptionally refreshing in the summertime, served well chilled with fresh, ripe mango.

BROWN SUGAR SYRUP

80 ml (2½ fl oz/⅓ cup) water
65 g (2¼ oz/⅓ cup) dark brown sugar

ALMOND JELLY

500 ml (17 fl oz/2 cups) almond milk
60 g (2 oz/scant ⅓ cup) caster (superfine) sugar
1½ teaspoons almond extract
½ teaspoon powdered agar or 1½ teaspoons agar flakes
1 ripe mango, peeled and diced, to serve

To make the brown sugar syrup, combine the water and dark brown sugar in a saucepan and bring to the boil. Stir to ensure the sugar has dissolved, then tip out into a bowl or container and transfer to the refrigerator.

In the same pan, combine the almond milk, sugar and almond extract and bring to the boil. Remove from the heat and whisk in the agar until completely dissolved.

Pour the mixture into 4 little dishes or cups, transfer to the refrigerator and leave to set and chill thoroughly – it should take about 4 hours.

Serve the almond jellies topped with the diced mango, with the brown sugar syrup drizzled over.

DIFFICULTY
Sublimely not difficult

NO-CHURN WHITE PEACH AND SAKE SORBET

SERVES 4–6 (MAKES ABOUT 400 ML/13 FL OZ/GENEROUS 1½ CUPS)

White peaches are the sexiest fruit: all juicy and blushing and fragrant, and they look like lovely, plump, furry bums. The ones grown in Japan are positively slutty, enormous and almost obscenely sweet. The fact that peach season is so short makes them all the more alluring, but with this recipe, you can preserve their intoxicating aroma for a few months longer by churning it into a slightly boozy sorbet. Sake seems to have a special affinity for peaches – in fact, some sake even have peachy notes themselves – and the alcohol helps keep this from setting too hard in the freezer. A scoop of this also tastes great in a glass of wheat beer, for a killer beer float to enjoy on a hot day.

4 big, ripe white peaches, stoned and diced
120 g (4 oz/scant ⅔ cup) caster (superfine) sugar
½ teaspoon vanilla extract
juice of 1 lemon
120 ml (4 fl oz/½ cup) sake (any will do, but a
    good-quality sake would be particularly nice)

Combine the peaches, sugar, vanilla and lemon juice in a container and leave in the refrigerator overnight.

In the morning, the sugar will have dissolved into a peachy syrup and the peaches themselves should be very soft. Add the sake and purée in a blender or food processor until smooth, then transfer to an airtight container and place in the freezer. Leave to freeze completely – it will take about 8 hours, maybe a little more or less depending on your freezer.

Enjoy immediately or store in the freezer for up to 3 months.

DIFFICULTY
Unimpeachably not difficult

SOY SAUCE BUTTERSCOTCH BROWNIES

I orginally developed this for Kikkoman, who wanted me to create non-Japanese recipes using soy sauce, to show people how it might be used in everyday cooking. For me it was great fun, because I love soy sauce and have always put it in everything anyway, but this was the first time I tried it in a dessert. It may sound like a silly gimmick but it really is delicious – there's a rich, malty, sort of stout-like flavour to soy sauce that works fantastically with chocolate and butterscotch. It's like salted caramel on steroids.

BUTTERSCOTCH

150 g (5 oz/¾ cup) light brown sugar
50 g (2 oz/3½ tablespoons) vegan butter
1 tablespoon vanilla extract
4 tablespoons soy sauce
4 tablespoons soy/almond/oat milk

BROWNIES

200 g (7 oz/generous ¾ cup) vegan butter
300 g (10½ oz) 60–80% dark chocolate, chopped
200 g (7 oz/1 cup) light brown sugar
80 g (3 oz/generous ⅓ cup) caster (superfine) sugar
4 tablespoons ground flaxseed combined with
    180 ml (6 fl oz/¾ cup) water or soy/almond/oat
    milk, or 4 eggs' worth of egg replacer, prepared
    according to the package instructions
100 g (3½ oz/¾ cup) plain (all-purpose) flour
30 g (1 oz/3½ tablespoons) cocoa powder
¼ teaspoon salt
icing (confectioner's) sugar, for dusting (optional)

To make the butterscotch, melt the sugar and vegan butter together in a saucepan over a medium heat, stirring frequently. When the sugar is dissolved and bubbly, add the vanilla, soy sauce and plant milk. Bring to the boil and cook for about 5 minutes, then remove from the heat.

Meanwhile, preheat the oven to 180°C (350°F/ Gas 6). Line a 30 × 20 cm (12 × 8 in) baking tray (pan) with baking parchment.

For the brownies, melt the vegan butter in a saucepan or in the microwave. Put the chocolate into a bowl, pour over the hot melted butter and stir together to melt the chocolate. Whisk in the sugars and flaxseed mixture or egg replacer. Sift in the flour, cocoa powder and salt, then stir everything together until no bits of flour remain.

Pour the brownie batter into the prepared tray and bake for 35-40 minutes. Shake the pan to check if the brownies are done - the middle should jiggle ever so slightly. Leave to cool completely before cutting into squares. Dust with icing sugar before serving, with the butterscotch on the side to pour over.

DIFFICULTY
Monumentally not difficult

CHOCOLATE MOUSSE WITH BOOZY CHERRIES AND MISO-ROASTED PECANS

SERVES 4

This recipe isn't Japanese, but I had to include it because I love the technique so much. It was invented as 'chocolate chantilly' by the chemist and food scientist Hervé This, who realised that a suspension of melted chocolate in water has the same kind of physical makeup as double (heavy) cream, so it can be whipped as such. The result is a fabulously light mousse that tastes of pure chocolate – because that's what it is. The richness of the mousse is balanced by cherries mixed with a bit of whisky, and the miso-roasted pecans add a fantastic salty-nutty crunch. I love this dessert because it looks quite retro, but the flavour is entirely modern.

MISO-ROASTED PECANS

15 g (⅔ oz/1 tablespoon) miso
1 teaspoon sesame oil
1 teaspoon caster (superfine) sugar
60 g (2 oz/generous ½ cup) pecan halves

MOUSSE

175 ml (6 fl oz/¾ cup) water
200 g (7 oz) dark (plain unsweetened) chocolate
1 teaspoon vanilla extract
ice, for chilling

TO FINISH

1 × 400 g (14 oz) tin cherry pie filling
4 tablespoons Japanese whisky or bourbon,
    or any not-too-smoky whisky

Preheat the oven to 160°C (320°F/Gas 4).

To make the miso-roasted pecans, mix together the miso, sesame oil and sugar in a bowl. Use your hands to coat the pecans with the miso mixture, then spread out on a baking sheet and roast for 10–15 minutes (check them after 10), until deep brown. Remove from the oven and leave to cool.

To make the mousse, bring the water to a simmer then add the chocolate and vanilla extract. Simmer until the chocolate is completely melted, then pour into a mixing bowl. Place this bowl inside another bowl half-filled with ice and a bit of water, then whisk the chocolate water as if you were whipping cream. As it cools it will thicken and aerate – stop whipping when the chocolate holds a trail, NOT when it forms peaks, because it is very easy to over-whip. However, if the mixture siezes up and goes grainy, you can just re-melt the chocolate and start over. Cool!

Scoop the mousse into glasses, ideally crystal so it all looks sufficiently 1970s. Stir the cherry pie filling together with the whisky, then spoon that on top of the mousse. Cover and refrigerate until 30 minutes before serving.

Garnish with the miso pecans just before tucking in.

DIFFICULTY
Deliriously not difficult

BLOODY MARIKO

SERVES 1

I have always loved Bloody Marys, because they are basically soup. I'm a terrible mixologist because I'm not very familiar with many spirits, nor proper cocktail technique, but I can make a damn good Bloody Mary because it's more like cooking – not far off tomato soup or gazpacho, really. This is a Japanese-flavoured version I made for Nanban a few years ago, which is really tasty, but unfortunately it never sold very well. The problem, I think, is that people associate them too strongly with brunch, and we don't serve brunch. Which is a shame, because this is really delicious, and it actually goes well with food. I guess because it kind of is food!

big pinch of shichimi, plus more for decorating
    glass rim (optional)
1 teaspoon soy sauce
1 teaspoon mushroom ketchup
½ teaspoon wasabi
100 ml (3½ fl oz/scant ½ cup) tomato juice
2 shots/3 tablespoons vodka or shochu
    (see note below)
juice of 1 lemon or 1 tablespoon yuzu juice
big pinch of black pepper
Tabasco or similar hot sauce, to taste
fresh raw crunchy veg (such as cucumber, celery,
    daikon, enoki mushrooms or chicory/endive),
    to garnish
ice cubes, to serve

Place a spoonful of shichimi on a plate, then wet the rim of a highball glass and dip it in the shichimi to make the shichimi rim.

Stir together the soy sauce, mushroom ketchup and wasabi until smooth, without any lumps of wasabi. Combine with all the other ingredients, except the garnish and ice, in a highball glass and stir well. Add the veg garnishes and enough ice cubes to fill the glass.

NOTE If you come across shochu, the Japanese distilled spirit, buy it! Its flavours range from clean and light, like a vodka or sake, to earthy and smoky, like mezcal or whisky – but shochu is typically much lower in alcohol than most spirits, around 25 per cent. Pretty much any shochu will work in this recipe, but I'd recommend a sweet potato or barley shochu, if you can find them.

DIFFICULTY
Bloody not difficult

デザートと飲み物   188   DESSERTS & DRINKS

WATERMELON SAKE MOJITO

Sake loves fruit (see also: No-Churn White Peach and Sake Sorbet, page 180) and I think it is especially nice with watermelon. I came up with this for a special 'summer of sake' promotion we ran at the restaurant a couple of years ago, and it was so popular it wound up on the permanent menu. It is really, really, really, stupidly refreshing. And really easy. And really pink!

½ lime, cut into little wedges, plus a slice of lime to garnish
3–4 cubes watermelon (seedless or deseeded)
1 teaspoon demerara sugar
10–12 mint leaves, plus an extra sprig to garnish
½ shot/1 tablespoon white rum
2 shots/3 tablespoons sake (try to use a nice fruity sake, if you can)
sparkling water, to top up
ice (ideally crushed), to serve

Muddle the lime, watermelon, sugar and mint together in the bottom of a highball glass until the watermelon is completely liquefied and the sugar is dissolved. Add the rum, sake, a splash of sparkling water and a handful of ice. Stir well and top with another splash of sparkling water.
    Garnish with a slice of lime and a sprig of mint and serve with a straw.

DIFFICULTY
So not difficult to make and even less difficult to drink

GREEN TEA BRANDY SLUSH

SERVES 4

A few years ago, I was rifling through old family recipe boxes back in Wisconsin, and I was amazed to find a few that were either Japanese dishes, or contained some kind of Japanese ingredient. Nothing too exotic – a bit of tempura here, some soy sauce there – but still, these were from the 1960s and 1970s. I had no idea anybody in Wisconsin was so adventurous. Then again, my Grandma Betty was not just anybody in Wisconsin. I didn't really know her – she died when I was four – but I gather she was a big personality, a fashionable and cosmopolitan woman who loved to entertain. So it made sense that she would have had a few recipes like this one in her collection, a kind of fusion cocktail that combines brandy slush – a Wisconsin supper club classic – with the fresh, grassy flavour of green tea.

4 x teabags of Japanese green tea, or 2 tablespoons loose-leaf Japanese green tea
180 ml (6 fl oz/¾ cup) brandy
500 ml (17 fl oz/2 cups) lemon sorbet (1 carton)
handful of crushed ice
juice of ½ lemon
4 slices of orange, to garnish

Steep the tea directly in the brandy, at room temperature – it should take 1–2 hours to infuse, but the longer you leave it the stronger it will taste.

Remove the teabags or strain out the leaves, and combine the infused brandy with the sorbet, ice and lemon juice in a food processor or blender and blitz until smooth and slushy.

Serve in snifters, garnished with orange slices.

DIFFICULTY
Wonderfully not difficult

GREEN TEA ARNOLD PALMER

The Arnold Palmer is one of the world's greatest drinks, a simple but highly effective combination of iced tea and lemonade (non-sparkling American lemonade, that is). The late golf legend for whom the drink is named preferred his made with three parts unsweetened tea to one part lemonade. I think this is about right – the lemon and sugar just sort of seasons the drink, making it more quenching but without interrupting the easy-going nature of iced tea. Green tea is a little more sharp than black tea, so I think it benefits from a little extra sweetness, but feel free to taste and adjust however you like. You can use any kind of Japanese green tea, but I quite like it with *hōjicha* (roasted tea) or *genmaicha* (toasted rice tea).

2 lemons
2 litres (70 fl oz/8 cups) water
80 g (3 oz/generous ⅓ cup) caster (superfine) sugar, or more to taste
8 x teabags of Japanese green tea, or 4 tablespoons loose-leaf Japanese green tea
ice cubes, to serve

Peel the lemons with a vegetable peeler, making sure there's as little white pith left on the peels as possible, then juice the lemons.

Place the lemon peels and the lemon juice in a saucepan with the water and sugar and bring to a simmer. Remove from the heat, leave to cool slightly, then add the tea. Leave to infuse for 5 minutes or so, or until it's as strong as you like it (add more sugar at this point as well, if you like).

Pass through a sieve (fine-mesh strainer) and chill in the refrigerator.

Serve in highball or pint glasses with plenty of ice.

DIFFICULTY
This is the last time I'll say it: it's not difficult

Tim Anderson is the proprietor of the Japanese soul food restaurant Nanban in London and the author of *Tokyo Stories*, *JapanEasy* and *Nanban*. He has studied Japanese cookery for two decades, and lived in Fukuoka prefecture for two years as a young man, immersing himself in Japan's highly diverse local food culture. He currently resides in Lewisham with his wife Laura, daughter Tig and FIV-positive cat Baloo. His favourite Marvel movie is *Captain America: Civil War*, but he also has a lot of love for *Spider-Man: Homecoming* and *Doctor Strange*.

ティムくん

Thank you Holly Arnold for making these books happen. And for dealing with people I don't want to deal with. And for the awesome knife you got me. You're the best.

Thank you Kate Pollard for your trust and your vision. This book, and the last two, are as much yours as they are mine and I hope you are as proud of them as I am.

Thank you Evi O. and Nassima Rothacker for making this book look far more beautiful than I ever could have imagined. You are both a true joy to work with and I'm so lucky to have you on the team.

Thank you Ruth Tewkesbury for your promotional wizardry. I am constantly impressed with the amount of press you and your team are able to generate for rice bowls and ramen.

Thank you Jackie Kearney for fielding my many vegan questions; *Vegan Street Food*, by the way, is still one of my favourite cookbooks ever.

Thank you Fumio Tanga, Patrick Knill, Emiko Pitman, Sam Schumacker and Yuki Serikawa for continuing to inspire and educate me in the many joys of Japanese cooking.

Thank you Laura for your love and support, and for continuing to tolerate and even encourage my many ridiculous pursuits.

Thank you Tig for being a constant fountain of joy.

Thank you Baloo for being the best friend I could ever hope for.

ACKNOWLEDGEMENTS

INDEX

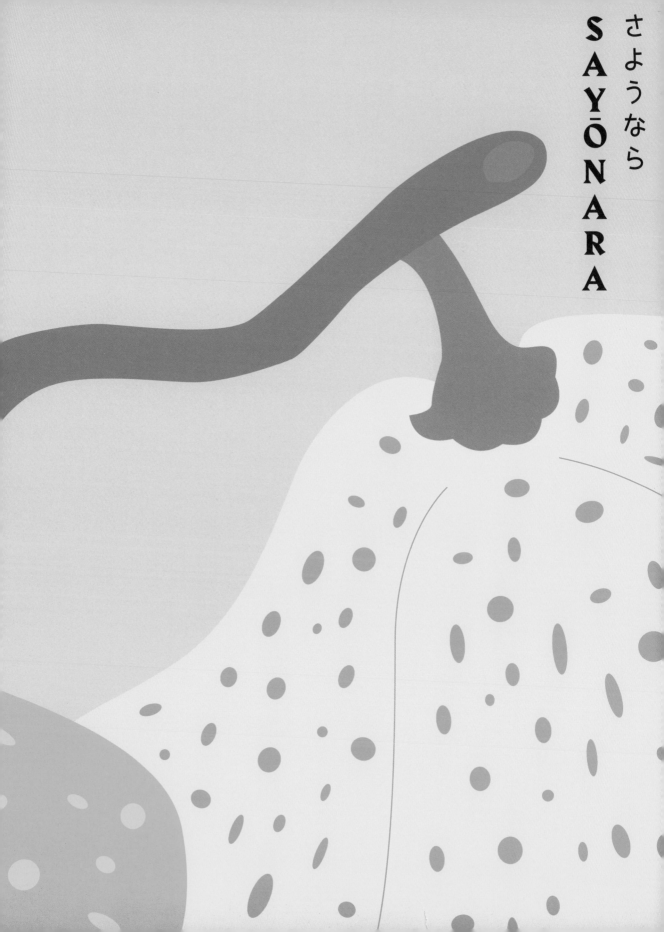

さようなら
SAYŌNARA

Published in 2019 by Hardie Grant Books,
an imprint of Hardie Grant Publishing

Hardie Grant Books (London)
5th & 6th Floors
52–54 Southwark Street
London SE1 1UN

Hardie Grant Books (Melbourne)
Building 1, 658 Church Street
Richmond, Victoria 3121

hardiegrantbooks.com

British Library Cataloguing-in-Publication Data.
A catalogue record for this book is available from
the British Library.

Vegan JapanEasy
ISBN: 978-1-78488-284-6

10 9 8 7 6

Publishing Director: Kate Pollard
Editor: Eila Purvis
Designer: Evi O. Studio | Evi O., Rosie Whelan, Nicole Ho
Photographer: Nassima Rothacker
Copy-editor: Emily Preece-Morrison
Proofreader: Lisa Pendreigh
Indexer: Cathy Heath

Colour reproduction by p2d
Printed and bound in China by Leo Paper Products Ltd.

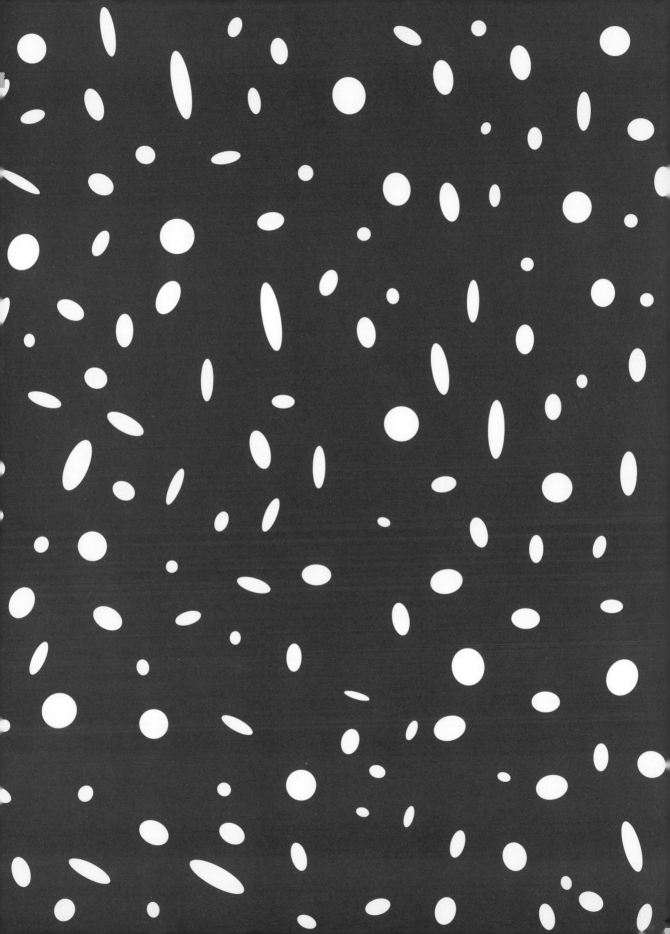